Written by **Kristina Tobutt**
With additional input by **Carmel Roche**

Editor: Linda Richardson
Designer: Tom Doyle

Special thanks to: Barbara Sudrow, Authentik

The Modern Languages in Primary Schools Initiative

Comhairle um Oideachas Gaeltachta agus Gaelscolaíochta

"… à la française" is produced by Authentik Language Learning Resources Ltd, a campus company of Trinity College Dublin, 27 Westland Square, Dublin 2, Ireland.

ISBN 978-1-905275-25-0

Authentik

List of Contents

"… à la française"   A Cross-curricular Approach to Teaching French at Primary Level   © Authentik

Using "... à la française"

"... à la française" is one of the first sets of resources that seek to address the aim of embedding the learning of French in the wider primary curriculum. All recent UK reports into language learning recommend this. It is also an aspect of EU educational policy.

It is not on policy grounds alone that these materials have been created. The rationale for this pack consists of a whole range of elements:

- that using 'survival' language alone is ultimately not sufficiently stimulating for learners whether the starting age is nine, seven or even five.

- that language learning is best achieved through **using language** as part of a **thinking process**.

- that language learning needs a **content** just as much as any other subject.

- that language learning should not be an add-on or peripheral part of a learner's experience but be included in and related to the **richness** of the whole curriculum.

- that **making connections** between what is learned through the mother tongue and what is learned in another language ultimately benefits the whole learning process by underpinning, revising and extending mental processes.

- that **intercultural content and activity** is crucial in making another language real.

When setting learning objectives for the teaching of elements of the primary curriculum in another language, we should think firstly of the non-language content. Language is also a major element of course; but we want to teach useful language and we want language to help the children, not to become a barrier. For these reasons the lesson plans here have both a content and a language focus.

The writers intend that the learners will leave the lessons knowing new facts or concepts in the subject area and that they will have used language in a meaningful way to do this. In using language like this they will also have learned useful vocabulary and phrases, which they will be able to apply to other related contexts.

Teaching in another language should not be so very different from everyday teaching in good primary settings. These resources have tried to build into this existing competence – if in doubt, trust your own good practice!

Where possible, presentation materials have been designed to engage the learners in noticing and thinking about new ideas. For example, primary teachers are often highly skilled in questioning techniques - here the teacher is encouraged to use simple questioning to establish both language and content rather than adopt a 'repeat after me' approach. To support this the teacher scripts show the scaffolding process and this is also recorded on the accompanying CD Rom. At the same time this form of modelling of a classroom language framework will, we hope, help teachers to design lessons on other topics themselves.

Independent work by children is also a part of these materials, even though the topics are 'tasters' rather than fully developed medium term lesson sequences. Children learning another language can always understand more than they can say or write and they can also think about more than they can express. We hope to stimulate them with the written word as well as with oral language and to encourage them to manipulate ideas as well as words.

Language learning should be fun and many of the activities in this pack are fun with an in-built challenge – meaningful fun!

How to use the materials

How do I use the cross-curricular materials?

For those teachers who have less experience of teaching French, the materials provide an excellent resource to familiarise themselves with the language needed to teach in a cross-curricular context. The native-speaker audio recordings will give you the necessary support before and during the lessons. Each unit comes with a detailed lesson plan and step-by-step activities, which will build up the language gradually. Teachers, who are already French specialists, might not need to rely as much on the audio recordings but will find the detailed unit plans useful to teach new content and concepts in order to adapt their teaching to a cross-curricular approach.

Many of the units come with a PowerPoint presentation that will help to structure your teaching. In addition these electronic materials will enrich your lessons with pictures and other resources to broaden the learners' cultural experience. Often the PowerPoint presentation is intended to follow an initial starter activity that activates the key vocabulary and ideas for the topic.

The lesson plans are designed to take 30-40 minutes. The follow-up activities are intended to allow you to do more during the rest of the week.

"... à la française"   A Cross-curricular Approach to Teaching French at Primary Level   © Authentik

Which units do I start with?

If you are a Primary school teacher with less experience at teaching French the easiest curriculum area to incorporate languages into your teaching might be Mathematics, especially as the pack contains several oral and mental starters which are easier to integrate in the earlier stages.

The materials also provide taster lessons in French from a wide range of commonly used primary topics. Most of the units are linked to a specific topic, such as Vikings, Victorian Children or Magnetism, which you may also be teaching in English parallel to using these lessons. Other units can be seen as free-standing units, such as some PE, music and maths lessons plans, which can easily be linked to a range of different topics.

How do I introduce each unit?

The lesson plans suggest ways to start the lesson in order to get all the children actively involved. They try to follow good primary practice by activating existing knowledge and engaging children immediately with simple decision-making or opinion giving, rather than through a repetition framework. (Where the latter technique is used there is an attempt to use physical actions and to move swiftly away from straightforward repetition to aural/oral-physical 'matching' i.e. the heard word to a movement or a movement to a spoken word).

Do the materials cater for all the children's needs?

As these are taster lessons rather than full units of work there is less differentiated material than would otherwise be the case. The teacher can choose whether to present all or part of the material and by copying the PowerPoint's or worksheets can adapt them, deleting or editing as appropriate.

The follow-up activities can be either used actively, giving children cards with words and images to manipulate or more abstractly through a written worksheet. In trialling the materials the teacher-author often used support either from herself or a teaching assistant to scaffold the participation of less able pupils.

We hope you enjoy and benefit from using these materials. We would be delighted to get your feedback and to learn about your experiences using this resource.

Please contact info@authentik.ie with "... à la française" in the subject line.

Kristina Tobutt

Mathématiques

Time guide: 30 minutes

Content: To reinforce basic 2D shapes and open-ended classification.
To practise giving a commentary on a transformation process.

Communication focus: To introduce or reinforce colours and
to introduce names of some 2D shapes.

Materials needed: A selection of different 2D shapes in different sizes and colours.

Links: Audio link – names of shapes and instructions.

Key Stage 2 Framework focus

O 3.4	Repeat words and phrases modelled by the teacher; remember a sequence of spoken words; use physical response, mime and gesture to convey meaning and show understanding
L 3.1	Read and understand simple messages
KAL	Imitate pronunciation; identify specific sounds, phonemes and words
LLS	Use actions and rhymes and play games to aid memorization
Languages Ladder	Stage 1 Breakthrough, Grade 2 Listening and Speaking
Irish Reference	Shape and space. Strand unit: 2D shapes

Transcription (CD Piste 1)

la forme :
un triangle
un cercle
un carré
un rectangle
un hexagone

la couleur :
bleu
rouge
vert
jaune
orange
violet

la taille :
grand
petit

Montrez-moi un triangle bleu !
Montrez-moi un cercle bleu !
Montrez-moi un cercle rouge !

Montrez-moi un petit triangle bleu !
Montrez-moi un grand cercle vert !

Montrez-moi un petit triangle bleu et un grand
cercle violet !

Classez les formes en groupes !
Je change de forme / de couleur / de taille.
Nous avons fini !

Lesson Plan:

1. Divide the class into groups and give each group a selection of shapes. Ask each group to hold up different shapes starting with cognates and primary colours.

Montrez-moi un triangle bleu !

Montrez-moi un cercle bleu !

Montrez-moi un cercle rouge !

Add the secondary colours. Once the children are familiar with the shapes and the colours, introduce the size.

Montrez-moi un petit triangle bleu !

Montrez-moi un grand cercle vert !

2. Now call out a variety of shapes, for example:

Montrez-moi un petit triangle bleu et un grand cercle violet !

3. Ask the children to sort the shapes into groups. Each group has to say how they divided up the pieces,

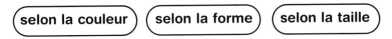

selon la couleur   selon la forme   selon la taille

4. The children are then asked to pick one shape, for example:

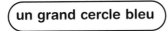

un grand cercle bleu

All the groups start with the same shape, then they have to add 10 more shapes, taking it in turns. They have to change one element each time, either the colour, the size or the shape. When they add their shape to the line, the children have to say one of the following:

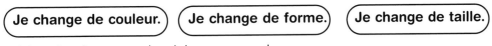

Je change de couleur.   Je change de forme.   Je change de taille.

When they have completed the sequence they say:

Nous avons fini !

5. Each group can hold up the final piece of their sequence and describe it. Check out if any groups ended up with the same.

Follow-up activities:

Step 4 can be extended by asking the children to start another sequence, this time they have to change two elements.

"... à la française" A Cross-curricular Approach to Teaching French at Primary Level © Authentik

Time guide: 10 to 15 minutes

Content: Calculating – add and subtract mentally combinations of one-digit and two-digit numbers.

Communication focus: Consolidation of numbers up to 60. Understanding and use of simple reasoning structures.

Materials needed: Magic square on whiteboard. Dominoes on tables. Copy master 1.2.

Links: Audio link – transcription of lesson

Key Stage 2 Framework focus:

O 3.3	Recall, retain and use vocabulary
L3.1	Identify and read simple words
KAL	Imitate pronunciation; identify specific sounds, phonemes and words
LLS	Use actions and play games to aid memorization
Languages Ladder	Stage 1 Breakthrough, Grade 2 Listening and Speaking
Irish Reference	Number. Strand unit: operations, add and subtract

Transcription (CD Piste 2)

Carré magique
Nous avons combien de lignes / combien de colonnes ? (trois)

Nous avons combien de diagonales ? (deux)

C'est combien, la somme de la première ligne ? (soixante)
Vingt-six plus dix-huit plus seize égale combien ?

C'est combien, la somme de la diagonale ? (soixante)
Vingt-six plus vingt plus quatorze égale combien ? (soixante)

Nous avons vingt-six plus dix, qu'est-ce qui manque ?
(vingt-quatre)

Pourquoi ? (Parce que la somme est soixante.)

Nous avons dix-huit plus vingt, qu'est-ce qui manque ? (vingt-deux).
Pourquoi ? (Parce que la somme est soixante)

Nous avons dix plus vingt, qu'est-ce qui manque ? (trente).
Pourquoi ? (Parce que la somme est soixante)

Quels sont les autres nombres qui manquent ?

Les nombres 1 à 60

+ plus

- moins

= égale

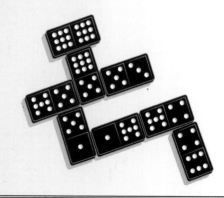

Lesson Plan:

1. Put the magic square on the whiteboard, or use Copy master 1.2. Start by asking some basic questions about the square, about the number of rows, columns and diagonals

> **Nous avons combien de lignes ? (trois)**

> **Nous avons combien de colonnes ? (trois)**

> **Nous avons combien de diagonales ? (deux)**

2. Ask the children to work out the sum of the first row,

> **C'est combien, la somme de la première ligne ?**

To reinforce the numbers go through the calculation

> **Vingt-six plus dix-huit plus seize égale combien ? (soixante)**

Follow the same steps with the diagonal

> **C'est combien, la somme de la diagonale ?**

> **Vingt-six plus vingt plus quatorze égale combien ? (soixante)**

Having looked at these two calculations, the children should now be able to deduce that the sums of each row, column and diagonal are the same

> **La somme de chaque ligne, chaque colonne et chaque diagonale est soixante.**

3. Now ask the children to work out the missing numbers

> **Nous avons vingt-six plus dix, qu'est-ce qui manque ? (vingt-quatre)**

Ask the children to give you the reason

> **Pourquoi ? (Parce que la somme est soixante.)**

Use the same questions for the other missing numbers

> **Nous avons dix-huit plus vingt, qu'est-ce qui manque ? (vingt-deux)**

> **Pourquoi ? (Parce que la somme est soixante.)**

and finally

> **Nous avons dix plus vingt, qu'est-ce qui manque ? (trente)**

4. Cut up the dominoes, Copy master 1.2, for pair or group practice of numbers including written forms.

As a follow-up activity the children could design their own magic squares.

Time guide: 10 to 15 minutes

Framework strand : Understanding shape - read and record the vocabulary of position

Communication focus: Consolidation of numbers up to 20 and the alphabet

Materials needed: Bag with multi-link cubes. Copy master 1.3

Links: Audio link – transcription of lesson

Key Stage 2 Framework focus:

O 3.2	Listen with care
O 3.3	Recall, retain and use vocabulary
KAL	Imitate pronunciation; identify specific sounds, phonemes and words
LLS	Use actions and play games to aid memorization
Languages Ladder	Stage 1 Breakthrough, Grade 1 Listening and Speaking
Irish Reference	Shape and Space. Strand unit: lines and angles.

Transcription (CD Piste 3)

un	J'ai un, deux, trois… cubes dans le sac.	Trouvez les cases sur le quadrillage.
deux		Coloriez les cases !
trois	Je prends un, deux… quinze cubes.	E8, E5, C2, D2, B5, B6, E2, E3, B7,
quatre	Il y a combien de cubes dans le sac ?	B8, C5, D5, E4, C8, D8.
cinq	Cinq.	Montrez-moi les feuilles !
six		On obtient le nombre 5.
sept	Je prends un, deux… treize cubes.	
huit	Il y a combien de cubes dans le sac ?	Maintenant travaillez avec un
neuf	Sept.	partenaire !
dix		
onze	Voici un quadrillage.	
douze	La lettre indique le code de la colonne,	
treize	par exemple B.	
quatorze	Le nombre indique le code de la ligne,	
quinze	par exemple 2.	
seize	La code pour la première case est B2.	
dix-sept		
dix-huit	Ecoutez bien !	
dix-neuf		
vingt		

1. Count the multi-link cubes while putting them in the bag (**un, deux, trois etc.**), encourage the class to join in. Take out a certain number of cubes, leave the rest in the bag. Ask the children to check how many you have taken out,

> Je prends un, deux, trois... cubes.

Start by taking out a higher number of multi-links in order to reinforce numbers. Then practise number bonds by asking the children how many are left in the bag,

> Il y a combien de cubes dans le sac ?

Ask a child to verify. Repeat these steps several times.

2. Give out the photocopied worksheets to practise coordinates and locate a shape on the grid. Model the position of the first square on the grid.

> Voici un quadrillage. La lettre indique le code de la colonne, par exemple B.

Point to the column on the grid.

> Le nombre indique le code de la ligne, par exemple 2.

Show the position of the first square on the grid,

> La code pour la première case est B2.

3. Now ask the children to record the position of the rest of the squares on the grid and colour them in.

> Ecoutez bien! Trouvez les cases sur le quadrillage. Coloriez les cases !

E8, E5, C2, D2, B5, B6, E2, E3, B7, B8, C5, D5, E4, C8, D8.
Ask the children to hold up the sheets to check the results,

> Montrez-moi les feuilles ! On obtient le nombre 5.

4. Use the other grids for pair practice of numbers and coordinates,

> Maintenant, travaillez avec un partenaire !

As a follow-up activity look at a map of a French town centre and locate the position of roads and public buildings. (See example)

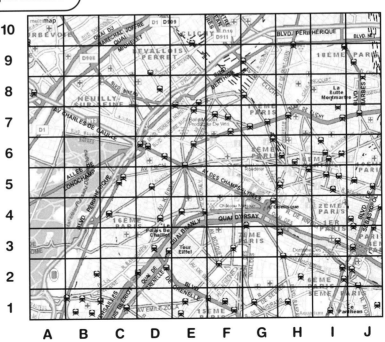

Mathématiques

Time guide:	10 to 15 minutes
Content:	Knowing and using number facts - multiplication
Communication focus:	Consolidation of numbers up to 40
Materials needed:	Soft ball, photocopied worksheet. Copy master 1.4
Links:	Audio link – transcription of lesson

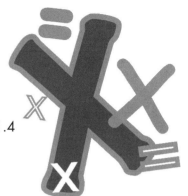

Key Stage 2 Framework focus

O 3.2	Listen with care
O 3.3	Recall, retain and use vocabulary
L 3.1	Identify and read simple words
KAL	Imitate pronunciation; identify specific sounds, phonemes and words
LLS	Use actions and play games to aid memorization
Languages Ladder	Stage 1 Breakthrough, Grade 1 Listening and Speaking
Irish Reference	Number. Strand unit: operations, multiplication

Transcription (CD Piste 4)

Ecoutez bien et répétez si vous avez la balle.

0, 4, 8, 12, 16, 20, 24, 28, 32, 36, 40

Qu'est-ce que j'ai dit ? C'étaient quels nombres ?
(les nombres, la table de multiplication de quatre).

Maintenant, nous allons compter : un, deux, trois...
Mais, attention ! Ne répétez pas les nombres quatre, huit, douze...
A la place nous allons dire 'lundi'.
Un, deux, trois, lundi !, cinq, six, sept, lundi !, neuf, dix, onze, lundi !, treize...

Levez-vous !
Mettez-vous en cercle !

Prenez les feuilles ! Trouvez les paires !

X fois
= égale

2 X 4 = 8
deux fois quatre égale huit

Lesson Plan:

1. Introduce the numbers of the 4 times table in French. Ask the children to listen carefully and repeat the words when it is their turn to throw the soft ball.

> **Ecoutez bien et répétez si vous avez la balle.**

Say one number at a time, then throw the soft ball and encourage the children to repeat while they throw the ball back to you.

> **Zéro, quatre, huit, douze, etc.**

Go back to zero to restart several times, building up the numbers gradually.
Ask the children which kind of words you have said:

> **Qu'est-ce que j'ai dit ? C'étaient quels nombres ?**

(les nombres, la table de multiplication de quatre).

2. Repeat the activity with soft ball, this time counting from 0 to 40. If they get to a multiple of 4 they must not repeat what you have said but say a previously agreed word (for example the day of the week, or describe the weather).

> **Maintenant, nous allons compter, un, deux, trois... Mais, attention ! Ne répétez pas les nombres quatre, huit, douze... A la place nous allons dire 'lundi'.**

Start to throw the ball, **un, deux, trois, lundi !, cinq, six, sept, lundi !, neuf etc**.

3. Ask the children to stand up, if possible in a circle.

> **Levez-vous ! Mettez-vous en cercle !**

Play the counting game as before, this time they have to count on without your help, so no repetition. As before they have to miss out all multiples of four. If they say a wrong number they have to sit down.

4. Use the worksheet for pair or individual practice of numbers and muliplication:

> **Prenez les feuilles ! Trouvez les paires !**

Change the activity to practice any other times tables.

1.5

Mathématiques

Time guide: 10 to 15 minutes

Content: Knowing and using number facts – derive and recall multiplication facts for the 3,4,5,6 and 8 times tables

Communication focus: Consolidation of numbers up to 100. Extending knowledge of mathematical language

Materials needed: Mini whiteboards and whiteboard markers. Copy master 1.5

Links: Audio link – transcription of lesson

Key Stage 2 Framework focus

O 4.2	Listen with care
L 4.2	Make links between the spoken and written words
KAL	Recognise patterns in simple sentences
LLS	Use context and previous knowledge to determine meaning and pronunciation
Languages Ladder	Stage 1 Breakthrough, Grade 2 Listening, Speaking and reading
Irish Reference	Number. Strand unit: operations, multiplication and division.

Transcription (CD Piste 5)

Les nombres 1 à 100

Je pense à un nombre.
On peut le diviser par cinq.
Ecrivez un nombre qu'on peut diviser par cinq !
Montrez-moi !

On peut le diviser par trois.
Ecrivez un nombre qu'on peut diviser par cinq et par trois !
Montrez-moi !

Il y a deux chiffres.
Le premier chiffre est trois.

Ecrivez un nombre !
On peut le diviser par cinq et par trois. Le premier chiffre est trois.
Montrez-moi !
C'est quel nombre ? (trente)

Maintenant, prenez les feuilles et travaillez avec un partenaire !

"... à la française"   A Cross-curricular Approach to Teaching French at Primary Level   © Authentik

Lesson Plan:

1. Give out mini whiteboards / sheets of paper and markers. For the first step of the activity the children can either work individually or in pairs.
Start by saying that you are thinking of a number,

> **Je pense à un nombre.**

Say that the number is divisible by 5 and ask the children to write a possible number on their whiteboards / sheets of paper.

> **On peut le diviser par cinq.**

> **Ecrivez un nombre qu'on peut diviser par cinq !**

Check the children's answers.

> **Montrez-moi !**

Give the next clue, say that the number is divisible by 3.

> **On peut le diviser par trois. Ecrivez un nombre qu'on peut diviser par cinq et par trois !**

Again, check the children's answers.

> **Montrez-moi !**

For the next clue, it is a two digit number, give visual support by putting two lines on the board.

> **Il y a deux chiffres.**

Then give the last clue, the first digit is 3, pointing to the line of the first digit.

> **Le premier chiffre est trois.**

Then ask the children to guess the number.

> **Ecrivez le nombre! On peut le diviser par cinq et par trois. Le premier chiffre est trois.**

Check the children's answers.

> **Montrez-moi ! C'est quel nombre ? (trente)**

2. Give out the photocopied worksheets for further practice.

> **Maintenant, prenez les feuilles et travaillez avec un partenaire !**

Working in pairs, the children complete two similar tasks.

3. In task three on the worksheet the children have to complete a numbers puzzle for each other, then swap and solve each other's.

4. Use task four as extension work.

15

1.6 Mathématiques

Time guide:	30 minutes
Content:	Using and applying mathematics – solve one step and two step problems involving money
Communications focus:	Consolidation of numbers up to 100 and the use of currency
Materials needed:	Envelopes with play money (euros) inside (if euro play money is not available, print and cut visuals), mini whiteboards and whiteboard marker. Copy master 1.6
Links:	Audio link – transcription of lesson

Key Stage 2 Framework focus

O 5.1	Ask and answer questions
L 4.4	Develop and perform simple role plays
IU 3.4	Make indirect or direct contact with the country/countries where the language is spoken
KAL	Use question forms
LLS	Practise new language with a friend and outside the classroom
Languages Ladder	Stage 1 Breakthrough, Grade 2 Listening and Speaking
Irish Reference	Measures. Strand unit: money

Transcription (CD Piste 6)

Voici les enveloppes.

J'ai un, deux, trois, quatre, cinq... quinze enveloppes.
Dans chaque enveloppe, il y a des euros.
Dans une, il y a un centime; dans une autre, il y a 10 centimes. Il y a une enveloppe avec un euro, cinquante euros ou cinq cents euros, par exemple.

Il faut payer 12 euros 50 centimes.
Je donne un billet de dix euros, une pièce de deux euros et une pièce de cinquante centimes.

Maintenant, prenez les feuilles et travaillez avec un partenaire !

Travaillez en groupes !

Enveloppe numéro quatre, s'il vous plaît !
Vingt euros.
Ecrivez ça au tableau.
Maintenant, ajoutez les centimes et les euros sur vos tableaux !
Vous avez combien d'euros ?
Vous avez gagné !

Jeu de rôle :

Bonjour ! Je voudrais des billets, s'il vous plaît !
C'est pour combien de personnes ?
Un adulte et deux enfants, s'il vous plaît.
Ça fait 116 euros, s'il vous plaît.
Voilà !
Merci !

"... à la française" A Cross-curricular Approach to Teaching French at Primary Level © Authentik

1. Prepare the envelopes before the lesson: put either a coin or a note in each of the envelopes, and then number them 1 to 15.
Start the lesson by holding up the envelopes and counting them.

> **Voici des enveloppes. J'ai un, deux, trois, quatre, cinq... quinze enveloppes. Dans chaque enveloppe, il y a des euros.**

Explain that there are different amounts of money in each envelope.

> **Dans une, il y a un centime; dans une autre, il y a 10 centimes. Il y a une enveloppe avec un euro, cinquante euros ou cinq cents euros, par exemple.**

Divide the class into groups. Each group needs to record the amount of money which they collect during the game on their mini whiteboard. One group at a time calls out the number of an envelope.

> **Enveloppe numéro quatre, s'il vous plaît !**

Open it and tell the group the amount inside, which the group then writes down on their whiteboard.

> **Vingt euros. Ecrivez ça au tableau.**

Continue with the next group. As the notes and coins emerge, place them in the right order on the board so children can see the pattern.

2. Once all the envelopes have been opened, ask the children to add up the amount they collected.

> **Maintenant, ajoutez les centimes et les euros sur vos tableaux ! Vous avez combien d'euros ?**

Each group calls out their amount, the group with the highest amount wins.

> **Vous avez gagné !**

3. For the next activity the children have to work out which coins and notes are needed to pay an exact amount. Model this first.

> **Il faut payer 12 euros 50 centimes.**

Write the amount on the board.

> **Je donne un billet de dix euros, une pièce de deux euros et une pièce de cinquante centimes.**

Hold up the notes and coins and stick them on the board.
Now use the Copy master 1.6 for pair practice.

> **Maintenant, prenez les feuilles et travaillez avec un partenaire !**

4. Go onto the Eurodisney website. http://offres.disneylandparis.fr/billets/index.xhtml
The children have to calculate how much a family of six has to pay.
As a follow-up activity the children can develop a short role play, asking for tickets. This time they could pretend to buy tickets for their own families.

> **Bonjour ! Je voudrais des billets, s'il vous plaît !**
> **C'est pour combien de personnes ?**
> **Un adulte et deux enfants, s'il vous plaît.**
> **Ça fait 116 euros, s'il vous plaît.**
> **Voilà !**
> **Merci !**

Mathématiques

Time guide:	10 to 15 minutes
Content:	Counting and understanding numbers
Communication focus:	Consolidation of numbers up to 110
Materials needed:	Mini whiteboards and whiteboard markers, counting stick
Links:	Audio link – transcription of lesson

Key Stage 2 Framework focus	
O 3.3	Recall, retain and use vocabulary
L 3.1	Identify and read simple words
LLS	Imitate pronunciation; identify specific sounds, phonemes and words
Language Ladder	Breakthrough, Grade 2 Listening and Speaking
Irish Reference	Number. Strand unit: place value, read, write and order numbers.

Transcription (CD Piste 7)

Prenez vos tableaux et écrivez les nombres !

Ecrivez un nombre entre dix et vingt.
Montrez-moi !
Ecrivez un nombre entre trente et quarante.
Montrez-moi !

Ecrivez un nombre entre quatre-vingts et
quatre-vingt-dix !
Montrez-moi

Maintenant, écrivez un nombre qui est plus grand
que cinquante ! > 50
Ecrivez un nombre qui est plus petit que
soixante ! < 60

sept
dix-sept
vingt-sept
trente-sept
quarante-sept
cinquante-sept
soixante-sept
soixante-dix-sept
quatre-vingt-sept
quatre-vingt-dix-sept
cent sept

Qu'est-ce que c'est ? (cinquante-sept)

"… à la française" A Cross-curricular Approach to Teaching French at Primary Level   © Authentik

Lesson Plan:

1. Give out the mini-whiteboards and pens and ask the children to write down certain numbers on the board.

> **Prenez vos tableaux et écrivez les nombres !**

First, ask the children to write down any number between 10 and 20.

> **Ecrivez un nombre entre dix et vingt !**

Use gestures or the counting stick to support comprehension. Keep revising the tens by using the same format of questioning:

> **Ecrivez un nombre entre trente et quarante. Montrez-moi ! Ecrivez un nombre entre quatre-vingts et quatre-vingt-dix !**

2. Introduce 'greater than' in your questions

> **Maintenant, écrivez un nombre qui est plus grand que cinquante !**

as well as 'smaller than'

> **Ecrivez un nombre qui est plus petit que soixante !**

Again, use the counting stick to support comprehension or write the greater than/smaller than symbols on the board.

3. Use the counting stick to count on in steps of 10, starting for example with 7. Encourage the children to join in

> **sept, dix-sept, vingt-sept, trente-sept, quarante-sept, cinquante-sept, soixante-sept, soixante-dix-sept, quatre-vingt-sept, quatre-vingt-dix-sept, cent sept**

With the counting stick count back in steps of ten.

> **Cent sept, quatre-vingt-dix-sept, quatre-vingt-sept, etc.**

4. Now use the counting stick to ask the children to identify a number part way along the stick, eg. point half way along the counting stick, ask

> **Qu'est-ce que c'est ? (cinquante-sept)**

Change the activity for further practice, starting with any other number.

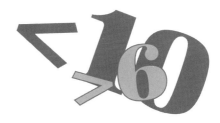

Time guide: 30 minutes + follow-up activities

Content: To develop cultural awareness of the
                     location *La Réunion* and to use and
                     interpret maps.

Communication focus: To introduce some geographical vocabulary
                     and to focus on question form *'Où est ..?'*

Materials needed: Powerpoint presentation *'Un papillon sur La Réunion'*,
                     a globe to locate the UK and *La Réunion*.

Links: Audio link – transcription of lesson
                     Visual link – powerpoint presentation, flashcards of geographical features
                     of the island.

Key Stage 2 Framework focus

O 3.1	Join in with storytelling
O 3.3	Recall, retain and use vocabulary
L 4.2	Make links between spoken and written words
IU3.2	Identify some of the countries where the language is spoken
KAL	Recognise question forms and negatives; identify specific sounds, phonemes and words
LLS	Use the context of what they see/read to determine some of the meaning
Languages Ladder	Stage 1 Breakthrough, Stage 2 and 3 Listening and Speaking
Irish Reference	People and other lands. Strand unit: study an environment in a non-European country

Transcription (CD Piste 8)

Où est la Grande - Bretagne ?
Où est l'Irlande ?
Où est l'Afrique ?
Où est Madagascar ?
Où est La Réunion ?

<u>Le papillon sur La Réunion</u>
p.2 : La Réunion est une île dans l'océan Indien.
p.3 : Bienvenue à la Réunion !
p.4 : « Bonjour ! Nous sommes les enfants de La
     Réunion. Où est le papillon ? »
p.5 : Où est le papillon ? Il est à la plage ?
     (Non !)

p.6 : Où est le papillon ? Il est dans la mer ?
     (Non !)
p.7 : Où est le papillon ? Il est dans la maison ?
     (Non !)
p.8 : Où est le papillon ? Il est à la montagne ?
     (Non !)
p.9 : Où est le papillon ? Il est dans le volcan ?
     (Non !)
p.10 : Où est le papillon ? Il est derrière la fleur ?
     (Oui, voilà !)

Lesson Plan:

1. Start by asking the children to locate Britain and Ireland on a globe:

> **Où est la Grande - Bretagne ?**   **Où est l'Irlande ?**

Continue with the following questions:

> **Où est l'Afrique ?**
>
> **Où est Madagascar ?**
>
> **Où est La Réunion ?**

2. Start powerpoint presentation, invite children to find the butterfly by asking:

> **Où est le papillon ?**

During the story the children meet some of the geographical features of the island both visually and through vocabulary items:

la plage   **la mer**   **la maison**   **la montagne**   **le volcan**

3. After the butterfly has been found show the map of the island again. Use the flashcards together with questions:

> **Où est la mer ?**
>
> **Où est la montagne ?**
>
> **Où est le volcan ?**
>
> **Où est la maison ?**

Invite children to come to the front and identify the visual representation of these features on the map. Stick flashcards on the map.

4. Look at the **La Réunion** children's drawings of their island and ask the learners to describe the pictures, using

> **Voici...............**

Follow-up activities:

Read the children's descriptions of their island. Look at an internet weather page (eg www.meteoconsult.fr) to compare climate with their own area.

2.2

Géographie

Time guide:	30 minutes + follow-up activities
Content:	Understanding and answering questions about countries in Europe
Materials needed:	Quiz. Copy master 2.2, photocopied map of Europe
Links:	Audio link – transcription of lesson

Key Stage 2 Framework focus

O 5.1	Ask and answer questions
L 4.2	Make links between spoken and written words
KAL	Imitate pronunciation of sounds; recognise patterns in simple sentences
LLS	Play games to remember; use context and previous knowledge to determine meaning and pronunciation
Languages Ladder	Stage 1 Breakthrough, Grade 3 Listening and Reading, Grade 2 Speaking
Irish Reference	A sense of place and space. Strand unit: develop an understanding of the names and relative location of some natural and human features of Europe and the world

Transcription (CD Piste 9)

Maintenant, nous faisons un quiz des pays en Europe.
Travaillez en groupes de trois.

Quiz :
Quel pays est situé entre l'Allemagne et l'Italie ? (l'Autriche)
Quel pays est situé au sud du Danemark ? (l'Allemagne)
Quel pays est situé au nord-est de la France ? (la Belgique)
Les deux pays qui ne touchent pas la France sont... (l'Irlande et l'Autriche)
Quel est le pays le plus grand ? (la France)
Quel est le pays le plus petit en Europe ? (le Luxembourg)
Quel pays a plus d'habitants que la France ? (l'Allemagne)
Les capitales de ces pays sont... (Paris, Bruxelles, Madrid)

Prenez les cartes et vérifiez vos réponses !

Je pense à un pays...
Le pays est au sud-ouest de la France.
Le pays est plus petit que la France.
Il y a moins d'habitants qu'en France.
La capitale est Lisbonne.
C'est quel pays ? (le Portugal)

Je pense à un pays....
Le pays est au sud/au nord/à l'est/à l'ouest de la France ?
C'est plus grand / plus petit que la France ?
Il y a plus d'habitants qu'en France ?
Il y a moins d'habitants qu'en France ?
La capitale est Berlin ?

"... à la française" A Cross-curricular Approach to Teaching French at Primary Level © Authentik

Lesson Plan:

1. Give out the quiz and let the children work in groups of three. The groups have to collaborate to deduce meaning of some unknown language and to generate previously learned facts about Europe. The multiple choice format of the quiz should support the children's comprehension of questions and introduce the names of the countries at the same time. The quiz includes questions about the location of different countries

> **Quel pays est situé entre l'Allemagne et l'Italie ? Les deux pays qui ne touchent pas la France sont...**

It uses some compass points

> **Quel pays est situé au sud du Danemark ? Quel pays est situé au nord-est de la France ?**

and asks about the size of countries

> **Quel est le pays le plus grand ? Quel est le pays le plus petit ?**

as well as population

> **Quel pays a plus d'habitants que la France ?**

and finally the capital cities of some countries

> **Les capitales de ces pays sont...**

2. Each group is given a map to verify and mark their answers.

> **Prenez les cartes et vérifiez vos réponses !**

Check children's comprehension by going through some of the questions of the quiz. Then adapt the questions, eg.

> **Quel pays est situé au nord-est de l'Espagne ?**

3. Play 'I am thinking of a country...'

> **Je pense à un pays...** Model this first by giving clues about a certain country.

> **Le pays est au sud-ouest de la France. Le pays est plus petit que la France. Il y a moins d'habitants qu'en France. La capitale est Lisbonne. C'est quel pays ? (le Portugal)**

Give the children one or two more examples before they start the questioning.

4. Start the next step of the game by saying
> **Je pense à un pays....**

Encourage children to ask questions which can only be answered with Oui/non, such as using the compass points or asking about the size of the country.

> **Le pays est au sud/au nord/à l'est/à l'ouest de la France ? C'est plus grand / plus petit que la France ?**

The children could ask about the population in comparison with France

> **Il y a plus d'habitants qu'en France ? Il y a moins d'habitants qu'en France ?**

or about the capital city
> **La capitale est Berlin ?**

The child who guessed the country correctly gets to choose the next country.

Follow-up activities:
the map can be used for more in depth comparison of the number of inhabitants.
For further detailed information about each country go on http://fr.wikipedia.org/wiki/France .
Simply replace 'France' by the country you wish to look at.

Time guide:	30 minutes + follow-up activities
Content:	Introduction to some buildings in Paris
Communication focus:	Basic geographical vocabulary
Materials needed:	Powerpoint presentation, Copy master 2.3, cut up facts about buildings in Paris (in envelopes)
Links:	Audio link – transcription of lesson Visual link – powerpoint presentation

Key Stage 2 Framework focus

O 4.2	Listen with care
L 4.1	Match phrases and short sentences to pictures and themes
IU4.4	Revise the location of country/countries where the language is spoken
IU5.2	Learn about buildings and places in different countries
LLS	Discuss language learning and share ideas and experiences; use context and previous knowledge to help understanding
Languages Ladder	Stage 1 Breakthrough, Grade 3 Reading and Listening, Grade 2 Speaking
Irish Reference	Human environments. Strand unit: become familiar with the names, locations and some well-known features of the capital cities of the European Union

Transcription (CD Piste 10)

p.1 Bienvenue à Paris !

p.2 Voici une planète. C'est la Terre.

p.3 Sur la Terre il y a des continents. C'est quel continent ? C'est l'Afrique/ l'Australie/ l'Amérique du Sud/ l'Europe/ l'Asie ? (Europe)

p.4 C'est quel pays ? C'est l'Espagne/ la France/l'Angleterre… ? (la France)

p.5 C'est quelle ville ? (Paris)

p.6 C'est quelle rue ? (les Champs-Elysees)

p.7 C'est quel monument/bâtiment ? (l'Arc de Triomphe)

p. 8 C'est quel monument/bâtiment ? C'est le musée du Louvre? C'est la Tour Eiffel ? C'est la Cathédrale de Notre-Dame ?

p. 9 C'est quel monument/bâtiment ?
Il a été construit en 1594.
Il y a plus de 8 millions de visiteurs par an.

La pyramide à l'entrée fait 21 mètres de haut.
C'est un musée.
Ici on peut voir La Joconde de Léonard de Vinci.

Levez la main si vous pensez que c'est la Tour Eiffel !
Levez la main si vous pensez que c'est le musée du Louvre !
Levez la main si vous pensez que c'est la Cathédrale Notre-Dame de Paris !

p.10 C'est le Louvre !

Travaillez en groupes !

Qu'est-ce que tu veux visiter ?
Pourquoi ? (Parce que j'aime l'art.)

Lesson Plan:

1. The first part of the powerpoint presentation gives an introduction into the location by gradually 'zooming' into the area, starting with

> **Voici une planète. C'est la Terre. Sur la Terre, il y a des continents.**

Develop questioning around each slide

> **C'est quel continent ? C'est l'Afrique/l'Australie/ l'Amérique du Sud/l'Europe/l'Asie ?,**
> **C'est quel pays ? C'est l'Espagne/ la France/l'Angleterre… ? C'est quelle ville ?**

2. Show the pictures of the three buildings in Paris, ask children to name them.

> **C'est quel monument ? C'est le musée du Louvre ? C'est la Tour Eiffel ? C'est la Cathédrale de Notre-Dame ?**

Continue with the description of one of the buildings and ask the children which one it is. Take a vote

> **Levez la main si vous pensez que c'est la Tour Eiffel !**
> **Levez la main si vous pensez que c'est le musée du Louvre !**
> **Levez la main si vous pensez que c'est la Cathédrale Notre-Dame de Paris !**

Reveal the answer. Discuss which clues the children used to make up their minds (eg. knowledge of previously learned language or cognates, such as **mètres, construit**).

3. Give out envelopes with words cut up from the Copy master. Ask the children to work in small groups matching the facts to each monument.

> **Travaillez en groupes !**

4. Check children's answers. Read out sentences and ask children to name the building described. Ask the children to decide which of the three buildings they would like to visit. For extension, encourage the children to give reasons

> **Qu'est-ce que tu veux visiter ? Pourquoi ? (Parce que j'aime l'art.)**

Follow-up activities:

Use the following websites to look at other places of interest in Paris.
www.paris.org/Monuments/
http://fr.wikipedia.org/wiki/Portail:Paris

Working in groups, the children could plan a day in Paris, visiting three different monuments.
Children write new words of the 'zooming-in' activity on cut out clouds (use two colours, write **une planète** on one colour and **la Terre** on the other one), attach pairs of vocabulary to string (in the order from big to small) and hang them up in the classroom.

2.4 Géographie

Time guide:	30 minutes + follow-up activities
Content:	To develop cultural awareness of the location La Réunion, contrasting weather conditions
Communication focus:	Weather, months and seasons
Materials needed:	Powerpoint presentation, printed and cut up months and seasons, a globe to locate Paris and La Réunion. Copy master 2.4
Links:	Audio link – transcription of lesson

Key Stage 2 Framework focus

O 3.3	Perform simple communicative tasks using single words, phrases and sentences
L 3.1	Recognise some familiar words in written form
L 4.2	Follow a short familiar text, listening and reading at the same time
IU3.2	Identify some of the countries where the language is spoken
IU5.2	Recognise similarities and differences between places
KAL	Notice the spelling of familiar words
LLS	Use context of what they see/read to determine some of the meaning
Languages Ladder	Stage 1 Breakthrough, Stage 2 Listening, Speaking, Reading and Writing
Irish Reference	Natural environments. Strand units: weather, climate and atmosphere

Transcription (CD Piste 11)

p.1 Paris et La Réunion:saisons et climat.

p.2 Nous sommes à Paris. Il y a du soleil. La température est de 30 degrés.
Nous sommes en juillet ou en décembre ? (juillet)
Nous sommes à La Réunion. Il y a du soleil. La température est de 30 degrés.
Nous sommes en juillet ou en décembre ? (décembre).
Pourquoi c'est différent ?
Où est Paris? Où est La Réunion ?
Paris est dans l'hémisphère Nord,
La Réunion est dans l'hémisphère Sud.

p.3 Les saisons – pour Londres et Paris – automne, hiver, printemps, été.
Quels sont les mois pour chaque saison ?
Les saisons – pour La Réunion.

Quels sont les mois pour chaque saison ?

p.4 Il y a d'autres différences ? Regardez les températures !
La température est plus élevée à Paris au mois de
.... et .... et
La température est plus élevée à La Réunion au mois de .... et .... et ....

p.5 En été, la température moyenne est de 29 °C le jour, et de 22°C la nuit.
Il pleut beaucoup.
Alors, ce sont quels mois ? (décembre, janvier, février)
En hiver, la température moyenne est de 24°C le jour, et de 17°C la nuit.
Alors, ce sont quels mois ? (juin, juillet, août)

Quel temps fait-il ? Il y a du soleil ? Il pleut ? Il y a du vent ?

"... à la française" A Cross-curricular Approach to Teaching French at Primary Level © Authentik

Lesson Plan:

Before the lesson, print and cut up the months and seasons on Copy master 2.4.

1. Start the powerpoint presentation with slide 1 to introduce the theme of the lesson **Paris et La Réunion : saisons et climat**. Move on to slide two and start the questioning about the contrasting locations **Paris** and **La Réunion**. Describe the weather conditions in Paris and ask the children which month it could be

> **Nous sommes à Paris. Il y a du soleil. La température est de 30 degrés. Nous sommes en juillet ou en décembre ? (juillet)**

Now do the same with weather conditions on the island of La Réunion

> **Nous sommes à La Réunion. Il y a du soleil. La température est de 30 degrés. Nous sommes en juillet ou en décembre ? (décembre)**

Ask the children why the months/seasons are different **Pourquoi, c'est différent ?** Explain the difference by looking at a globe or the satellite picture of the world. Ask the children to find the two locations **Où est Paris ? Où est La Réunion ?** Get the children to deduce that Paris is in the northern hemisphere whereas La Réunion in the southern hemisphere **Paris est dans l'hémisphère Nord, La Réunion est dans l'hémisphère Sud.**

2. Move on to slide 3 to describe the seasons for London and Paris

> **Les saisons – pour Londres et Paris – automne, hiver, printemps, été.**

Give out the cards and, working in small groups, ask the children to allocate the months to the correct seasons **Quels sont les mois pour chaque saison ?** Do the same for **La Réunion** to demonstrate the meaning of the different hemispheres **Les saisons – pour La Réunion. Quels sont les mois pour chaque saison ?**

3. To reinforce the contrasting climates, ask the children to look at the temperature diagrams on slide 4 **Il y a d'autres différences ? Regardez les températures !** Working in pairs, the children find the hottest months in Paris as well as in **La Réunion. La température est plus élevée à Paris au mois de .... et .... et ....**
La température est plus élevée à La Réunion au mois de .... et .... et ......

4. Move on to slide 5 to reinforce the concept of the different seasons on La Réunion. Summarise the weather during the summer months : **En été, la température moyenne est de 29 °C le jour, et de 22°C la nuit. Il pleut beaucoup.** Ask the children to give you the months **Alors, ce sont quels mois ? (décembre, janvier, février).** Then do the same asking for the winter months : **En hiver, la température moyenne est de 24°C le jour, et de 17°C la nuit. Alors, ce sont quels mois ? (juin, juillet, août).** Show the graph to verify the answers.
Finally, look at another weather phenomenon, the cyclones. Ask the children to describe the weather in the two pictures : **Quel temps fait-il ? Il y a du soleil ? Il pleut ? Il y a du vent ?**

5. Give out Copy master 2.4 to reinforce description of weather graphs.
For an extension activity print out slide 6 of the powerpoint and get children to find out some record weather facts in Paris.

Follow-up activities:
Look at the phenomenon of cyclones. Here are some useful websites:
www.la.climatologie.free.fr/cyclone/cyclone.htm#cycl1
www.ac-reunion.fr/pedagogie/cotamarp/temps/climat/cyclone.html
www.meteo.fr/temps/domtom/La_Reunion/

Keep a weather diary over a certain period of time and compare the weather in your area with the weather in France.

3.1

Musique

Time guide:	30 minutes + follow-up activities
Content:	Musical instruments of an orchestra
Communication focus:	Expressing likes and dislikes of musical instruments
Materials needed:	Powerpoint presentation, Copy master 3.1
Links:	Audio link – transcription of lesson Visual link – powerpoint presentation

Key Stage 2 Framework focus

O 5.2	Understand and express likes and dislikes
L 6.1	Read and understand the main points and some detail from a short written passage.
KAL	Recognise patterns in simple sentences; manipulate language by changing an element in a sentence.
LLS	Apply knowledge about letters and simple grammatical knowledge to experiment with writing; integrate new language into previously learnt language; look and listen for visual and aural clues.
Languages Ladder	Stage 1 Breakthrough, Grade 3 Listening, Speaking and Reading, Grade 2 Writing
Irish Reference	Listening and responding to music: Exploring sound. Identify families of instruments. Distinguish the main instrument heard in a piece of music.

Transcription (CD Piste 12)

Les instruments de l'orchestre

p.2 C'est quel instrument ? C'est le violon.

p.3 C'est quel instrument ?
C'est la flûte ?

p.4 C'est quel instrument ?
C'est la trompette ?

p.5 Voici un plan de l'orchestre.
Les instruments à cordes sont le violon, le violoncelle et la contrebasse.
Dans le groupe des bois, il y a la flûte, le hautbois, la clarinette et le basson.
Dans le groupe des cuivres, il y a le cor, la trompette et le trombone.
Dans le groupe des percussions, il y a la grosse caisse, les timbales ou le tambour et les cymbales.

C'est dans quel groupe ? Dans le groupe des cordes, des bois, des cuivres ou des percussions ?

Quels sont ces instruments ?
Quels instruments sont dans le groupe des percussions, des cuivres, des cordes et des bois ?
Choisis la même couleur pour chaque groupe et ses instruments.
J'adore le son de...
J'aime aussi le son de...
Je déteste le son de...
Je voudrais jouer de...
Je joue déjà de...

Maintenant, comparez vos avis avec un partenaire !

"... à la française" A Cross-curricular Approach to Teaching French at Primary Level   © Authentik

Lesson Plan:

1. Start the powerpoint presentation Les instruments de l'orchestre. Introduce some instruments by showing the visuals on the next slide **C'est la contrebasse, le cor, la grosse caisse et le violon.**

Now ask the children to identify the sound of three of the instruments. Click on the speaker icons and ask the children

> **C'est quel instrument ?**

Children reply by naming the correct instrument **C'est le violon**.
Do the same with the next two slides

> **C'est quel instrument ? C'est le cor, la clarinette, le trombone ou la flûte ? C'est quel instrument ? C'est la clarinette, le hautbois, le violoncelle ou la trompette ?**

2. Move on to slide 5 to introduce the seating plan of an orchestra

> **Voici un plan de l'orchestre.**

Read the text, go through each group of instruments and point to their place within the orchestra.

> **Les instruments à cordes sont le violon, le violoncelle et la contrebasse. Dans le groupe des bois, il y a la flûte, le hautbois, la clarinette et le basson. Dans le groupe des cuivres, il y a le cor, la trompette et le trombone. Dans le groupe des percussions, il y a la grosse caisse, les timbales ou le tambour et les cymbales.**

3. For further practice of identifying and naming musical instruments click on the speaker icons and ask the children to name which group of instruments they belong to

> **C'est dans quel groupe ? Dans le groupe des cordes, des bois, des cuivres ou des percussions ?**

Then in the next step try to identify the instruments **Quels sont ces instruments ?**

(Additionally, copy and cut Copymaster 3.1 asking the children to match the instrument name and picture, and then to group them.)

4. Give out Copy master 3.1. The first task is reinforcing the different groups of instruments

> **Quels instruments sont dans le groupe des percussions, des cuivres, des cordes et des bois ?**

The children can colour-code each group as shown on the powerpoint

> **Choisis la même couleur pour chaque groupe et ses instruments.**

The second task is designed to practise and reinforce likes and dislikes. The children express which sounds of musical instruments they like or dislike : **J'adore le son de... J'aime aussi le son de... Je déteste le son de...**
In addition they are asked to say which instruments they would like to play or play already : **je voudrais jouer de... Je joue déjà de...** Draw their attention to the changing form of **du/de la/des**. Ask individuals if they can identify the pattern (masculine/feminine/plural).

5. Ask the children to compare their opinions with another person at their table.
Maintenant, comparez vos avis avec un partenaire !

Follow-up activity:
Conduct a survey to find the most popular instrument in the class. **Quel est l'instrument le plus populaire dans la classe ?** The children can either say which instrument they would like to play **Je voudrais jouer de...** or name the one which they already play **Je joue déjà de...**

3.2

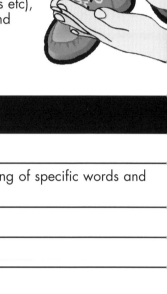

Time guide: 30 minutes + follow-up activities

Content: Percussion instruments and sound effects

Communication focus: Describing weather

Materials needed: Copy master 3.2, materials for rain stick: cardboard tube (empty kitchen towel roll), some seeds (or rice, beads etc), some cardboard and paper, sticky tape, hammer and nails (shorter than the diameter of the tube), paint to decorate

Links: Audio link – transcription of lesson

Key Stage 2 Framework focus

O 4.1	Learn finger rhymes, poems or a non-fiction text
O 4.2	Use physical response to show recognition and understanding of specific words and phrases
L 4.2	Make links between spoken and written words
KAL	Develop accuracy in pronunciation and intonation
IU 5.2	Identify geographical features of contrasting locality
LLS	Practise new language with a friend; read and memorise words; use actions and rhymes to aid memorisation
Languages Ladder	Stage 1 Breakthrough, Grade 2 Listening, Speaking and Reading
Irish Reference	Listening and responding. Strand unit: explore ways of making sound using manufactured and home made instruments

Transcription (CD Piste 13)

Aujourd'hui nous allons créer le son d'un cyclone sur La Réunion.
Nous allons utiliser les mains, les doigts, les jambes et les pieds.

Ecoutez et faites comme moi !

Le vent s'approche. Ecoutez !
La pluie commence.
Il pleut plus fort.
Le cyclone fait rage !

Le cyclone se calme.
Il pleut moins fort.
La pluie s'arrête.
Le vent s'en va. Ecoutez !

Maintenant, travaillez en groupes de quatre.
Utilisez les phrases et les actions pour créer le son.

<u>Un bâton de pluie</u>
Matériel: un rouleau en carton
          des graines
          du carton ou du papier
          du scotch
          un marteau et des clous
1. Prends le rouleau en carton. Prends le marteau. Plante les clous dans le rouleau.
2. Bouche un coté du rouleau avec un morceau de carton en forme de rond (au diamètre du rouleau).
3. Mets des graines dans le rouleau. Bouche l'autre côté du rouleau avec un deuxième morceau de carton en forme de rond.
4. Décore le bâton de pluie.

Lesson Plan:

This lesson can be linked to the Geography units on La Réunion. If you have not taught these units use some visuals of the island, preferably in contrasting weather conditions, including a cyclone.

1. Start the lesson by introducing the theme. Tell the class that they are going to create the sound of a cyclone on the island of **La Réunion**

> **Aujourd'hui nous allons créer le son d'un cyclone sur La Réunion.**

They are going to use their hands, their legs and their feet to recreate the sound

> **Nous allons utiliser les mains** (hold up hands), **les doigts** (hold up and wiggle fingers), **les jambes** (touch legs) **et les pieds** (touch feet).

2. Ask the whole class to listen and copy your actions **Ecoutez et faites comme moi !**

Say that the wind is approaching and rub your palms **Le vent s'approche. Ecoutez !**

The whole class joins in. Then the rain starts, click your fingers

> **La pluie commence.**

Again, the whole class joins in. The rain gets stronger, tap your hands on your legs **Il pleut plus fort**

Finally, the cyclone is there, tap your feet on the floor **Le cyclone fait rage !**

3. Split the class into four groups, each group will create one of the sound effects. Start with the first group

> **Groupe 1 : Le vent s'approche. Ecoutez !**

and build up the sound gradually until all groups are involved

> **Groupe 2 : La pluie commence. Groupe 3 : Il pleut plus fort. Groupe 4 : Le cyclone fait rage !**

Then the cyclone calms down

Le cyclone se calme.   Group 4 stops tapping their feet.

Il pleut moins fort.   Group 3 stops tapping their hands.

La pluie s'arrête.   Group 2 stops clicking their fingers.

Le vent s'en va. Ecoutez !   Group 1 stops rubbing their palms.

4. Split the class, so the children work in groups of three to recreate the same effects. Give out worksheets for support. **Maintenant, travaillez en groupes de quatre. Utilisez les phrases et les actions pour créer le son.** The children say the phrase matching their sound : **Le vent s'approche etc.**

5. Ask groups to present to the whole class.

Follow-up activity:
Make a rain stick. Follow instructions on worksheet 'Un bâton de pluie'.
1. Take cardboard tube and insert nails with the hammer.
2. Cover one end of the tube with cardboard.
3. Fill the tube with the seeds. Cover the other end of the tube with cardboard.
4. Decorate the rain stick!

3.3

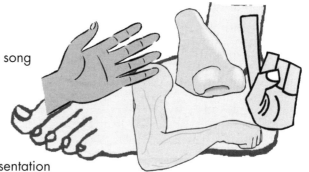

Time guide: 30 minutes

Content: To learn a traditional French song

Communication focus: Parts of the body

Materials needed: None

Links: Audio link – song
Visual link – powerpoint presentation

Key Stage 2 Framework focus	
O 3.1	Listen and respond to simple rhymes, stories and songs
KAL	Identify specific sounds, phonemes and words
LLS	Use actions and rhymes and play games to aid memorisation
Languages Ladder	Stage 1 Breakthrough, Grade 2 Listening and Speaking
Irish Reference	Listening and responding to music. Strand unit: singing

---

Transcription (CD Piste 14)

<u>Ecoutez, répétez et faites comme moi !</u>
la main
le doigt
le pied
le genou
le coude
le nez

<u>Fermez les yeux !</u>
Ecoutez bien. Touchez le nez. Touchez le coude. Levez la main. Levez le doigt. Touchez le genou. Touchez le pied.

<u>Savez-vous planter les choux ?</u>
Savez-vous planter les choux ?
à la mode, à la mode.
Savez-vous planter les choux
à la mode de chez nous ?

(la main)
On les plante avec la main
à la mode, à la mode.
On les plante avec la main
à la mode de chez nous.

(le doigt)
On les plante avec le doigt
à la mode, à la mode.
On les plante avec le doigt
à la mode de chez nous.

(le pied)
On les plante avec le pied
à la mode, à la mode.
On les plante avec le pied
à la mode de chez nous.

(le genou)
On les plante avec le genou
à la mode, à la mode.
On les plante avec le genou
à la mode de chez nous.

(le coude)
On les plante avec le coude
à la mode, à la mode.
On les plante avec le coude
à la mode de chez nous.

(le nez)
On les plante avec le nez
à la mode, à la mode.
On les plante avec le nez
à la mode de chez nous.

Lesson Plan:

1. In this lesson the children will learn some parts of the body through a traditional French song

(**Savez-vous planter les choux ?**)

Do you know how to plant cabbage? This can be linked to any science unit on plants or growth or used as a freestanding unit.

2. Start by teaching the parts of the body. Ask the children to repeat and copy your actions after each new word

(**Ecoutez, répétez et faites comme moi !**)

Hold up one hand and say (**la main**)

Then hold up one finger and say (**le doigt**)

Touch one foot and say (**le pied**)

Then touch a knee and say (**le genou**)

Touch an elbow and say (**le coude**)

Finally touch your nose and say (**le nez**)

Repeat the body parts in a different order several times. Once the children have practised the new words several times, ask them to close their eyes while touching the parts of the body which you call out

(**Fermez les yeux ! Ecoutez bien. Touchez le nez. Touchez le coude. Levez la main. Levez le doigt. Touchez le genou. Touchez le pied.**)

3. Play the song and ask the children to listen for the parts of the body and perform the actions as before when they hear them.

4. Now teach the song. Use the powerpoint for visual support. Play the first verse and ask the children to join in

(**Chantez !**)

Before each new verse, remind the children of the part of the body coming which is coming up

(**la main**)

(hold up one hand), play the verse and ask the children to join in.

5. Now ask the children to find a partner to sing the song and perform the actions with a partner. While they are singing the song, the children have to use the correct part of the body to touch each other in the rhythm of the song: hand to hand, finger to finger, foot to foot, knee to knee, elbow to elbow and finally, carefully touch each other's nose with one finger. Get volunteers to perform in pairs.

4.1

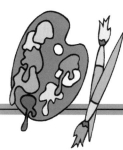

Time guide: 30 minutes + follow-up activities

Content: Paper collages by Henri Matisse

Communication focus: Describing art, analysing colour and form

Materials needed: Powerpoint presentation

Links: Audio link – transcription of lesson
Visual link – powerpoint presentation

Key Stage 2 Framework focus

O 4.2	Listen with care; show physical response to show recognition and understanding of specific words and phrases
L 6.1	Read and understand the main points from a short written passage
KAL	Recognise patterns in simple sentences
LLS	Integrate new language into previously learnt language; look and listen for visual and aural clues
Languages Ladder	Stage 1 Breakthrough, Grade 3 Listening, Speaking and Reading
Irish Reference	Paint and Colour. Strand Unit: looking and responding

Transcription (CD Piste 15)

p.1 Henri Matisse

p.2 Henri Matisse est né le 31 décembre 1869 et est mort le 3 novembre 1954.
C'était un peintre, dessinateur et sculpteur français.
En 1943, il a commencé à faire des collages.
Il a utilisé une technique spéciale : la technique des gouaches découpées.

p.3 C'est quel animal ?
C'est un chat ?
C'est un loup ?
C'est un chien ?
Je pense que c'est un loup.
Pourquoi ?
Parce qu'il a les dents pointues. Parce qu'il est féroce.

p.4 C'est quel animal ?
C'est un poisson ?
C'est un chat ?
C'est un escargot ?
Je pense que c'est un escargot.

p.5 Quelles sont les trois couleurs primaires ? Jaune, bleu et rouge.
Les couleurs primaires sont les couleurs qui ne peuvent pas être composées par d'autres couleurs.

p.6 Quelles sont les trois couleurs secondaires ? Vert, orange et violet.
Les couleurs secondaires sont composées par deux couleurs primaires.
Par exemple, bleu et jaune font quelle couleur ? Vert.

p.7 Les couleurs complémentaires sont opposées sur le cercle chromatique.

p.8 Quelle est la couleur complémentaire du jaune/vert/orange ?

p.9 Quelles sont les couleurs primaires dans L'Escargot ?
Quelles sont les couleurs secondaires ?
Quelles sont les couleurs complémentaires ?

p.10 Il y a des formes droites…
Il y a des formes arrondies…

p.11 Quelles sont les formes droites ? Quelles sont les formes arrondies ?

p.12 Discutez avec un partenaire.
Quelles sont les couleurs primaires ou secondaires ?
Quels sont les contrastes ?
Les formes jaunes sont des oiseaux, des étoiles ou des plumes ?

"… à la française"   A Cross-curricular Approach to Teaching French at Primary Level   © Authentik

Lesson Plan:

1. Start the powerpoint presentation Henri Matisse. Go to slide 2 to find out some background information about Matisse. You could do this as a whole class activity or as paired reading. Move on to slide 3 to introduce one of Matisse's paper collages, The Wolf. Ask the children to identify the title of the collage by asking which animal is being portrayed

> **C'est quel animal ? C'est un chat ? C'est un loup ? C'est un chien ?** Children reply **Je pense que c'est un chat/un loup/un chien.** Encourage children to give reasons : **Pourquoi ? Parce qu'il a les dents pointues. Parce qu'il est féroce.**

Move to slide 4 to show the picture of The Snail and follow the same steps as before.

> **C'est quel animal ? C'est un poisson ? C'est un chat ? C'est un escargot ?**

2. Start analysing the use of colours by distinguishing between primary and secondary colours. On slide 5 ask the children to identify and name the primary colours

> **Quelles sont les trois couleurs primaires ? Jaune, bleu et rouge.**

Then show the definition of primary colours, that they are pure colours which can not be made up by a mix of other colours.

> **Les couleurs primaires sont les couleurs qui ne peuvent pas être composées par d'autres couleurs.**

On slide 6 ask the children to identify and name the secondary colours

> **Quelles sont les trois couleurs secondaires ? Vert, orange et violet.**

Again, look at the definition of secondary colours

> **Les couleurs secondaires sont composées par deux couleurs primaires** and demonstrate an example **Par example, bleu et jaune font quelle couleur ? Vert.**

3. Move on to slide 7 to introduce the term of complementary colours. Show and discuss the definition

> **Les couleurs complémentaires sont opposées sur le cercle chromatique.**

The arrows demonstrate that complementary colours are opposite each other on the colour circle.
Ask the children to identify the complementary colours on slide 8

> **Quelle est la couleur complémentaire du jaune/vert/orange ?**

Ask volunteers to come to the board and show the contrasting colours on the colour circle while naming them.

4. Now analyse the use of colour in the picture The Snail. Ask children to identify primary, secondary and complementary colours

> **Quelles sont les couleurs primaires dans L'Escargot ? Quelles sont les couleurs secondaires ? Quelles sont les couleurs complémentaires ?**

and discuss that complementary colours create contrasts in the picture.
Then look at the use of contrasting shapes in this picture. Distinguish between straight and curvy shapes
Il y a des formes droites… Il y a des formes arrondies… Again, ask the children to find them in the picture
Quelles sont les formes droites? Quelles sont les formes arrondies ?

5. Working in pairs the children should then apply their knowledge of colours and contrasting forms to discuss another picture, Icarus. **Discutez avec un partenaire. Quelles sont les couleurs primaires ou secondaires ? Quels sont les contrastes ? Les formes jaunes sont des oiseaux, des étoiles ou des plumes ?**
Finish the lesson by asking each pair how they interpreted the yellow shapes in the collage.

Follow-up activity:
Look at the animated analyis of the The Snake on the Tate website
www.tate.org.uk/imap/pages/animated/cutout/matisse/snail.htm
The links in the powerpoint presentation take you to websites about Matisse and some of his paper collages. Check these websites for further information about the artist's life or try to look at other examples of his work.

4.2 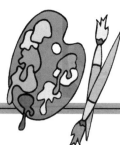 Arts

Time guide: 30 minutes + follow-up activities

Content: Making paper collages in the style of Henri Matisse

Communication focus: Understanding and following instructions

Materials needed: Powerpoint presentation, visuals and instructions cut up, water colour and paper, scissors, glue. Copy master 4.2

Links: Audio link – transcription of lesson
Visual link – powerpoint presentationn

Key Stage 2 Framework focus

O 4.2	Listen with care; show physical response to show recognition and understanding of specific words and phrases
L 4.1	Match phrases or sentences to pictures or themes
KAL	Recognise patterns in simple sentences; manipulate language by changing an element in a sentence.
LLS	Integrate new language into previously learnt language; look and listen for visual and aural clues.
Languages Ladder	Stage 1 Breakthrough, Grade 2 Listening, Speaking and Reading
Irish Reference	Paint and Colour. Strand unit: Painting. Exploring colour with a variety of colour drawing instruments, media and techniques

Transcription (CD Piste 16)

Aujourd'hui, nous allons faire des collages à la manière d'Henri Matisse.
Travaillez en groupes.
Trouvez les paires!

p.1 Prends le papier et la boîte de peintures.
Colorie le papier.

p.2 Prends les ciseaux.
Découpe des formes droites et des formes arrondies.

p.3 Avec toutes les formes, fais ta composition.
Prends la colle. Colle les formes sur du papier.

p.5 Et voilà, c'est fini !

Tu as des couleurs primaires ou secondaires ?
Tu as des couleurs complémentaires ?
Tu as des formes droites ou arrondies ?
Où sont les contrastes ?

Qu'est-ce que c'est ? C'est une maison/un arbre/un soleil...

"... à la française" A Cross-curricular Approach to Teaching French at Primary Level © Authentik

Lesson Plan:

1. Explain that the children are going to make their own paper collages in the style of Henri Matisse.

> **Aujourd'hui nous allons faire des collages à la manière d'Henri Matisse.**

Give out envelopes with the visuals and instructions of the process of making a collage from Copy master 4.2. Working in small groups, the children have to find the matching pairs

> **Travaillez en groupes. Trouvez les pairs!**

2. Start the powerpoint presentation a la manière d'Henri Matisse to demonstrate the process of making a collage. The children check if they matched pictures and instructions correctly.

> **Prends le papier et la boîte de peintures. Colorie le papier. Prends les ciseaux. Découpe des formes droites et des formes arrondies. Avec toutes les formes, fais ta composition. Prends la colle. Colle les formes sur du papier. Et voilà, c'est fini !**

3. Collect in the envelopes and set up the tables for the art work. Give out the materials needed and slowly go through the instructions while the children are working.
During the process go around and try to encourage children to talk about the process. Keep reminding them of the importance of thinking carefully about the use of colours and shapes by asking them

> **Tu as des couleurs primaires ou secondaires ? Tu as des couleurs complémentaires ? Tu as des formes droites ou arrondies ? Où sont les contrastes ?**

4. Once they have finished, ask the children to discuss their work with a partner. They describe the colours and shapes in each other's collages or ask for clarification

> **Qu'est-ce que c'est ? C'est une maison/un arbre/un soleil...**

Follow-up activities
Prepare an exhibition with the title Les collages à la manière d'Henri Matisse and ask the children to write labels with the titles of their collages or short descriptions in French.

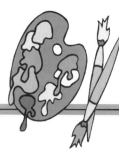

Time guide:	30 minutes + follow-up activities
Content:	Competition: designing a model of a bridge
Communication focus:	Language of instructions
Materials needed:	Materials for building the bridges: 4 sheets of A4 paper, 4 sheets of A4 card, 15 drinking straws, scissors and sticky tape per group. Copy master 4.3
Links:	Audio link – transcription of lesson

Key Stage 2 Framework focus

O 5.3	Understand the main points from speech which includes unfamiliar language
L 5.4	Memorise and present a set of instructions
KAL	Recognise patterns in simple sentences
LLS	Plan and prepare – analyse what needs to be done to carry out a task
Languages Ladder	Stage 1 Breakthrough, Grade 3 Listening, Speaking, Reading (Writing as follow-up activity)
Irish Reference	Construction. Strand unit: *explore and experiment with the properties and characteristics of materials in making structures.*

Transcription (CD Piste 17)

Concours : Faites un pont !

Aujourd'hui vous allez faire un projet.
Vous allez faire la maquette d'un pont.

Voici les instructions.

Faites un pont en groupes de quatre.

Vous avez 4 feuilles de papier,
4 feuilles de carton,
15 pailles,
des ciseaux,
du scotch.

Vous allez utiliser quels matériels ? Discutez et choisissez !

Décidez : le pont est en bois, en fer ou en pierre ?
Le pont est pour les véhicules ou pour les piétons ?

En groupe, lisez et discutez les instructions.

Maintenant, faites la maquette !

Attention !
Quand vous avez fini, vérifiez la stabilité de votre pont.
Placez une balle de tennis sur le pont – le pont est cassé, oui ou non ?

Lesson Plan:

1. Show the class an envelope with the details of the competition inside. Open it up and take out the sheet, copy master 4.3. Explain to the class that they are going to take part in a competition:

> **Concours : Faites un pont ! Aujourd'hui vous allez faire un projet. Vous allez faire la maquette d'un pont. Voici les instructions.**

Put the details up on the whiteboard and share them with the class.

2. Discuss the different steps of the competition with the class. Firstly, the children have to get into groups of four

> **Faites un pont en groupes de quatre.**

Then they find out which materials they are allowed to use

> **Vous avez 4 feuilles de papier, 4 feuilles de carton, 15 pailles, des ciseaux, du scotch.**

Hold up the materials. They have to discuss which of these materials they are going to use

> **Vous allez utiliser quels matériels ? Discutez et choisissez !**

They have to decide if the bridge is made of iron, wood or stone and if it is for vehicles or people

> **Décidez : le pont est en bois, en fer ou en pierre ? Le pont est pour les véhicules ou pour les piétons ?**

3. Divide the class into groups of four. Give out the worksheets with the instructions for the competition. Ask the children to read the instructions again and discuss their plan

> **En groupe, lisez et discutez les instructions.**

Each group gets a set of materials from which they can choose as many as they like. Once they have agreed on a plan for their design they can build the model

> **Maintenant, faites la maquette !**

4. Once they have finished, each group needs to test their bridge: take a tennis ball, let it roll across the bridge to check if it collapses or not

> **Attention ! Quand vous avez fini, vérifiez la stabilité de votre pont. Placez une balle de tennis sur le pont – le pont est cassé, oui ou non ?**

5. Each group presents their bridge to the rest of the class. Encourage children to describe it

> **C'est la maquette d'un pont de bois. C'est pour les piétons.**

Follow-up activity:
Take a vote to decide which group is the winner of the competition.

Time guide:	30 minutes + follow-up activities
Content:	To learn how and when the Vikings invaded France.
Communication focus:	Imperatives. To understand and give instructions, ranging from simple classroom instructions to Viking commands.
Materials needed:	Powerpoint presentation 'Les Vikings en France', a map of Europe to locate the Vikings' countries of origin and the countries which were invaded
Links:	Audio link – imperatives/classroom commands, story Visual link – powerpoint presentation

Key Stage 2 Framework focus

O 3.4	Repeat words and phrases modelled by the teacher; use physical response, mime and gesture to convey meaning and show understanding
L 4.2	Make links between spoken and written words
KAL	Imitate pronunciation of sounds
KAL	Use actions and rhymes and play games to aid memorization; use a physical response; use context of what they see/read to determine some of the meaning
Languages Ladder	Stage 1 Breakthrough, Grade 3 Listening and Reading, Grade 2 Speaking, Grade 2 Writing
Irish Reference	Early peoples and ancient societies. Strand unit: develop a balanced understanding of history and an appreciation of the contribution of different ethnic groups to history

Transcription (CD Piste 18)

<u>Les actions</u>

Ecoutez !
Regardez !
Levez-vous !
Levez le doigt !
Asseyez-vous !
Tout le monde à bord !
Ramez !
Attaquez !

<u>Une histoire des Vikings</u>

p.1	Les Vikings en France
p.2	Il était une fois un village au Danemark.
p.3	« Ecoutez ! Je m'appelle Rollo et j'habite au Danemark. Voici mon bateau, le drakkar. »
p.4	« Tout le monde à bord ! » Dans le village on dit « au revoir ».
p.5	« Ramez ! » Les Vikings voyagent sur des drakkars. Ils rament et rament et rament.
p.6	En 896, les Vikings arrivent en France. « Attaquez ! »
p.7	Les Vikings attaquent les villages et massacrent les habitants.
p.8	« Tu as peur ? » ; « Non, je n'ai pas peur. » ; « Attaquez ! »
p.9	Je m'appelle Rollo et je viens du Danemark. Mais j'habite en France maintenant.
p.10	Rollo et les Vikings restent en France.
p.11	En 911, le roi de France leur donne un territoire... la Normandie.
pp.12-18	Version de l'histoire avec des blancs

Lesson Plan:

1. Revisit or introduce simple classroom commands, ask the children to copy words and actions.

Ecoutez ! *(hand to ear)*

Regardez ! *(hand to eyes and point to object)*

Levez-vous ! *(stand up, gesture children to copy)*

Levez le doigt ! *(hold index finger up in the air)*

Asseyez-vous ! *(sit down)*

Practise a few times, then call out imperatives and ask children to give physical response.

2. Introduce Viking commands,

Tout le monde à bord ! *(gesture for all aboard)*

Ramez ! *(rowing action)*

Attaquez ! *(pretend to hold sword up in the air)*

Follow same steps as in 1. This can be extended by a game of **Jacques a dit** (Simon says).

3. Start powerpoint presentation, ask children to join in with actions when they hear any of the commands practised in 1 and 2.

4. Continue the powerpoint presentation, going through the story again. Invite the children to fill in the missing   words for language practice and an opportunity to assess comprehension.

5. Discuss the origin of the word Normandie, as the territory which the Vikings (the men from the North, the Normans) invaded and where they settled.

Follow-up activities:

Look at a map of Europe and locate Viking countries, **le Danemark, la Suède, la Norvège**.
Follow Viking routes and find some of the countries they invaded, **l'Angleterre, l'Irlande, la France**.

5.2

Histoire

Time guide:	30 minutes + follow-up activities
Content:	Viking artefacts and everyday objects. Viking markets.
Communication focus:	Je voudrais... Tu voudrais...? (language of bartering)
Materials needed:	Powerpoint presentation 'Aux temps des Vikings', Printed visuals of Viking artefacts worksheet. Copy master 5.2
Links:	Audio link – transcription of powerpoint Visual link – powerpoint presentation

Key Stage 2 Framework focus

O 3.3	Ask and answer questions
L 4.2	Make links between spoken and written words
KAL	Imitate pronunciation of sounds, recognise conventions of politeness
LLS	Practise new language with a friend, and outside the classroom
Languages Ladder	Stage 1 Breakthrough, Grade 3 Listening and Reading, Grade 2 Speaking, Grade 2 Writing
Irish Reference	Early peoples and ancient societies. Strand unit: develop a balanced understanding of history and an appreciation of the contribution of different ethnic groups to history

Transcription (CD Piste 19)

Les objets des Vikings

une broche
une cuillère
une épée
un vase
un bateau
un collier
un peigne
un verre
des chaussures

Aux temps des Vikings

p.1 Aux temps des Vikings
p.2 Les Vikings avaient-ils du chocolat ? (Non)
p.3 Les Vikings avaient-ils des épées ? (Oui)
p.4 Les Vikings avaient-ils des bijoux ? (Oui)

p.5 Les Vikings avaient-ils la télévision ? (Non)
p.6 Les Vikings avaient-ils des peignes ? (Oui)
p.7 Les Vikings avaient-ils des cuillères ? (Oui)
p.8 Les Vikings avaient-ils des trains ? (Non)
p.9 Les Vikings avaient-ils des verres ? (Oui)
p.10 Qu'est-ce que c'est ?
p.11 Qu'est-ce que c'est ? Une épée ou une broche ?
p.12 Qu'est-ce que c'est ? Une épée ou un vase ?
p.13 Qu'est-ce que c'est ? Un bateau ou des chaussures ?

Au marché des Vikings

Tu voudrais une épée ?

Oui, s'il te plaît.

Non, merci.
Non, je n'en veux pas.

Donne-moi un peigne.
Oui, si tu me donnes une broche.

"... à la française"   A Cross-curricular Approach to Teaching French at Primary Level   © Authentik

esson Plan:

. Start the powerpoint presentation. Going through each slide the children decide which everyday objects existed during the time of the Vikings. Children respond to the questions with **Oui ou non**, focusing on the content rather than learning the new words. Cognates of today's objects should be easily comprehensible.

. Point to visuals to practise the words of Viking artefacts. Use actions to accompany words. Start by giving the children the option of two:

C'est une broche ou une épée ?

. Give out the pictures of Viking artefacts, Copy master 5.2, one set of pictures to 4 or five children. In order to familiarise themselves with the names of the objects, ask the children to hold up the pictures – introducing the form **'Je voudrais......'**.
Call out

Je voudrais un bateau.

Je voudrais un peigne.

Je voudrais des chaussures.

and check the children are holding up the correct visuals etc.

. Working in groups, the children pretend to have a Viking market. Model the conversation with one or two volunteers.

Tu voudrais des chaussures?

« Oui, s'il te plaît! » ; « Non, je n'en veux pas. »

For extension the children can add phrases like:

« Donne-moi un peigne ! » ; « Oui, si tu me donnes une broche. »

allowing them to add extra creativity to the role play situation. While they are swapping the objects, the children fill in the record sheet. Copy master 5.2.

. Return to the powerpoint presentation to play Devinez ! (guess the hidden object). Step by step reveal the hidden objects. Give the children the option of two.

Qu'est-ce que c'est ?

C'est une broche ou une épée ?

Follow-up activities:
Make a display of Viking objects with French labels.

Time guide:	30 minutes + follow-up activities
Content:	Child labour in France during the 19th century
Communication focus:	Expressions of emotions
Materials needed:	Powerpoint presentation. Copy master 5.3
Links:	Audio link – transcription of lesson Visual link – powerpoint presentation

Key Stage 2 Framework focus

O 5.1	Use tone of voice and gesture to help to convey meaning
L 6.1	Read and understand the main points from a short written passage
IU5.1	Reflect on cultural issues using empathy and imagination to understand other people's experiences
IU5.2	Learn about buildings and places in different countries
LLS	Integrate new language into previously learnt language; use actions and rhymes to aid memorisation; look and listen for visual and aural clues; compare the language with English
Languages Ladder	Stage 2 Preliminary, Grade 4 Listening, Speaking and Reading
Irish Reference	Life, society, work and culture in the past. Strand unit: life in the 19th century

Transcription (CD Piste 20)

p.1 Les enfants du 19ème siècle

p.3 Pendant longtemps, les enfants pauvres travaillaient comme les adultes.
Ils travaillaient dans les usines et dans les mines.

p.4 Les conditions de travail étaient horribles.
Les enfants commençaient á travailler à partir de 8 ou 9 ans.
« Quel âge as-tu ? » ; « J'ai neuf ans. »
Ils travaillaient jusqu'à douze heures par jour.
« Je suis fatigué ! »

p.5 Les enfants étaient moins payés que les adultes.
Le salaire :
un adulte – 2 francs par jour
          (une femme 1 franc)
un enfant – 45 centimes

A Mulhouse, en 1835, le pain coûtait 15 centimes, le lait 15 centimes et la viande de bœuf 45 centimes la livre.

p.6 Le travail dans les mines était dangereux, il y avait beaucoup d'accidents.

p.7 Qu'est-ce qu'il pense ?
Je suis fatigué !
J'ai chaud !
J'ai faim !
J'ai soif !
J'ai peur ! Le travail est dangereux.
Je veux jouer avec mes amis !

Before the lesson, print and photocopy the second slide of the powerpoint presentation. Ask the children to work in pairs to read and discuss the text, highlighting all the language they understand. Ask children for feedback in English and discuss the role of cognates (adultes, enfants, machines, mines, accidents) in unknown texts. Ask the children to read the text again to see if they can deduce the meaning of some unfamiliar language from the context, eg.
travail, travailler is mentioned several times in the text, can we guess what it means?

Start the powerpoint presentation. The same text is split into smaller chunks, now using visuals to support understanding. Slide 3 gives examples of some of the areas in which the majority of poor children were working.

> **Pendant longtemps, les enfants pauvres travaillaient comme les adultes. Ils travaillaient dans les usines … et dans les mines.**

Slide 4 highlights some of the working conditions for children

> **Les conditions de travail étaient horribles. Ils commençaient á travailler à partir de 8 ou 9 ans. Les enfants travaillaient jusqu'à douze heures par jour.**

Slide 5 exemplifies one of the reasons why children were used in factories and mines, the lower pay.

> **Les enfants étaient moins payés que les adultes.**

Slide 6 mentions the problems of accidents as another area of the poor working conditions.

> **Le travail dans les mines était dangereux, il y avait beaucoup d'accidents.**

Move onto slide 7 of the powerpoint presentation, which introduces some of the emotional language needed to express the child's feelings.
Go through the different phrases, using expression, mime and gesture to support understanding.
Start with
> **Je suis fatigué !** miming tiredness. Encourage children to join in with language and actions

> **Répétez et faites comme moi !**

Do the same with the other phrases

> **J'ai chaud ! J'ai faim ! J'ai soif ! J'ai peur ! Le travail est dangereux ! Je veux jouer avec mes amis.**

Practise a few times until the children are familiar with the language. Then invite volunteers to mime the action, another child has to say the phrase.

Give out Copy master 5.3 and ask the children to fill in boxes, demonstrating empathy with the child's possible feelings. The worksheet includes some additional phrases, some of which should not be used.

> **Ecrivez les phrases ! Attention ! On n'a pas besoin de toutes les phrases !**

As an extension activity, encourage children to think of questions which they would like to have asked the child. This could be done either in English or in French.

> **Quel âge as-tu ? Où est ta mère ? Où habites-tu ? As-tu des jouets ? As-tu des amis ?**

Follow-up activities:

For a more detailed study of children's living conditions in France during the 19th century try to explore the following websites :
www.droitsenfant.com/19siecle.htm" http://www.droitsenfant.com/19siecle.htm
http://juniors.chez-alice.fr/dossiers/enfants_19/enfants_19.htm
http://freinet.org/creactif/blain/cm/2004/exposes/enfants19.htm

5.4

Time guide:	30 minutes + follow-up activities
Content:	Child labour in France during the 19th century
Communication focus:	Use rhyme and rhythm to memorise language
Materials needed:	Powerpoint presentation, softball, Copy master 5.4
Links:	Audio link – transcription of powerpoint Visual link – powerpoint presentation

Key Stage 2 Framework focus

O 5.1	Use tone of voice and gesture to help to convey meaning
O 4.3	Listen for sounds, rhyme and rhythm
L 4.2	Make links between spoken and written words
IU5.1	Reflect on cultural issues using empathy and imagination to understand other people's experiences
LLS	Use actions and rhymes to aid memorisation
Languages Ladder	Stage 1 Breakthrough, Grade 3 Listening, Speaking and Reading
Irish Reference	Life, society, work and culture in the past. Strand unit: life in the 19th century

Transcription (CD Piste 21)

<u>Les enfants du 19ème siècle. Un poème.</u>

Trouve les paires qui riment.

usine	usine, machine
chaîne	nuit, bruit
chaud	chaîne, humaine
nuit	
humaine	chariot, chaud
machine	
bruit	
chariot	

<u>Un poème</u>

Tourne, machine, tourne jour et nuit.
Tourne, machine, tourne trop trop de bruit !

Pousse, garçon, pousse ton chariot.
Pousse dans la mine dangereuse ;
if fait chaud !

Rêve, enfant, rêve, enfant en chaînes.

Rêve, enfant, rêve, d'une vie plus humaine !

Lisez le poème avec un partenaire !

Lesson Plan:

1. Start the powerpoint presentation **Les enfants du 19ème siècle. Un poème.** Ask the children to find the matching pairs which rhyme.

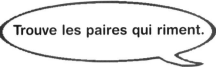

Trouve les paires qui riment.

Read words, then encourage children to read aloud the matching pairs. Move onto the next slide to verify answers.

2. For further pronunciation practice take a softball, throw it to a child while saying one of the words. Ask the child to say the matching rhyming word while throwing it back to you.

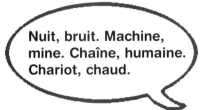

Nuit, bruit. Machine, mine. Chaîne, humaine. Chariot, chaud.

3. Start the first part of the poem on slide 4. Agree on an action which illustrates the turning wheels of a machine.

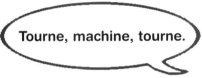

Tourne, machine, tourne.

Practise several times. Listen to the rest
Move onto the second part of the poem. Encourage the children to join in with an action which demonstrates a boy pushing a wagon in a mine.

Pousse, garçon, pousse.

For the last part of the poem agree on an action which illustrates a child dreaming.

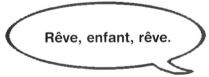

Rêve, enfant, rêve.

Practise these three phrases and actions until the children can say them confidently. Listen to the whole poem and ask children to join in with language and actions at the appropriate time.

4. Divide the class in three groups, allocate each part of the poem to one group and ask children to practise their part with a partner.
Finish the lesson by getting the whole class to perform the poem with the actions.

Follow-up activities:
Use the Copy master 5.4 to reinforce rhyme and rhythm of the poem in written form. In task 1 the children have to find the matching pairs. The second task is a gap fill activity.

You might want to discuss the problem of child labour which still exists in some countries even today.
To read authentic poems written by French children on the theme of child labour visit the following websites:
www.momes.net/Journal/poemes7/letravaildesenfants.html
www.ilo.org/public/french/standards/ipec/wdacl/2006/suzuki/suzuki.htm

Education physique

6.1

Time guide:	30 minutes
Content:	Parachute games
Communication focus:	Responding to instructions
Materials needed:	Parachute
Links:	Audio link – instructions to play the games

Key Stage 2 Framework focus

O 3.4	Use physical response, mime and gesture to convey meaning and show understanding
KAL	Identify specific sounds, phonemes and words
LLS	Use actions and rhymes and play games to aid memorization
Languages Ladder	Stage 1 Breakthrough, Grade 2 Listening
Irish Reference	Games. Strand unit: creating and playing games. Move more effectively and to interact with others.

Transcription (CD Piste 22)

<u>Echauffement</u>
Marchez lentement !
Marchez plus vite !
Courez lentement !
Courez plus vite !
Stop !

Asseyez-vous en cercle !

banane
poire
pomme
ananas
raisin
orange
fraise
citron

Tenez le parachute d'une seule main.
Marchez en rond !
Marchez plus vite !
Changez de main et courez dans l'autre direction !

<u>Changez tous !</u>
Levez le parachute !
Changez de place les bananes !
Changez de place les pommes et les oranges !
Changez de place les fruits jaunes !

Changez de place les anniversaires en janvier !
Marchez plus vite !
Baissez les bras !
Courez autour du parachute, pas au-dessous !

<u>Champignons</u>
Un, deux, trois, levez les bras !
Levez le parachute au-dessus de la tête et asseyez-vous !

"... à la française"   A Cross-curricular Approach to Teaching French at Primary Level   © Authentik

Lesson Plan:

1. For a warm-up activity, ask the children to move around the hall, increasing the speed gradually,

> **Marchez lentement !   Marchez plus vite !   Courez lentement !   Courez plus vite !   Stop !**

2. Ask the children to sit in a circle,

> **Asseyez-vous en cercle !**

and give each child the name of a fruit, an animal, a shape or any vocabulary practised recently. For example,

> **banane, poire, pomme, ananas, raisin, orange, fraise, citron**

The children will have to remember their allocated word(s) for the rest of the lesson.

3. Take the parachute and ask the children to hold on to it with one hand **Tenez le parachute d'une seule main.** Repeat the movements from 1, now with the parachute

> **Marchez en rond ! Marchez plus vite ! Courez lentement !**

Ask the children to change hands and directions

> **Changez de main et courez dans l'autre direction !**

4. Play **Changez tous !** Ask the children to lift the parachute up

> **Levez le parachute !**

Then call out fruits (colours, animals, shapes, numbers etc. - whichever items of vocabulary you decided to practise). The names of fruits can be used in a variety of ways. Firstly you can call out specific fruits and ask the children to run under the parachute and swap places

> **Changez de place les bananes !**   Ask for more than one fruit to swap

> **Changez de place les pommes et les oranges !**

then include colours   > **Changez de place les fruits jaunes !**

This game can be extended by a variety of instructions, for example by calling out birthday months

> **Changez de place les anniversaires en janvier !**

For a more energetic version of the game ask the children holding on to the parachute to walk fast

> **Marchez plus vite !** and keep the arms down

> **Baissez les bras !**

The children who are swapping places have to run around the outside of the parachute, not underneath

> **Courez autour du parachute, pas au-dessous !**

5. To finish play **Champignons**. On the count of three the children raise their arms, lifting the parachute over their heads and sitting down underneath the parachute

> **Un, deux, trois, levez les bras ! Levez le parachute au-dessus de la tête et asseyez-vous !**

Education physique

Time guide:	30 minutes
Communication focus:	To respond to instructions
Materials needed:	None
Links:	Audio link – instructions to play the game

Key Stage 2 Framework focus

O 4.2	Use physical response, mime and gesture to convey meaning and show understanding
KAL	Identify specific sounds, phonemes and words; engage in turn taking
LLS	Use actions and rhymes and play games to aid memorization; use gestures to show they understand
Languages Ladder	Stage 1 Breakthrough, Grade 2 Listening
Irish Reference	Athletics. Strand unit: develop a better understanding of speed, strength, control and co-ordination.

Transcription (CD Piste 23)

Courez lentement !
Courez plus vite !
Stop !

Aujourd'hui, nous sommes des Vikings.
Ecoutez bien et faites comme moi !

Attaquez !
Ramez !
Nettoyez le bateau !
Videz le seau !
Prenez vos boucliers !
Trouvez deux (trois, quatre…) Vikings !
Tout le monde à bord !

Courez lentement ! Nettoyez le bateau !
Et courez lentement ! Ramez !
Courez lentement ! Tout le monde à bord !

Travaillez en groupes de quatre.
En groupes, faites une séquence de quatre ou cinq actions.
Maintenant, présentez vos séquences.

Lesson Plan:

1. This unit can be used as a warm-up activity or a whole lesson. It can be linked to the history units on Vikings. Ask the children to run slowly around the hall, increasing the speed gradually, then slowing down again

> Courez lentement ! Courez plus vite ! Courez lentement ! Stop !

2. Explain to the children that they are going to pretend to be Vikings and that they have to follow your commands

> Aujourd'hui nous sommes des Vikings. Ecoutez bien et faites comme moi !

Introduce the commands and demonstrate the corresponding actions one by one. Start with

> Attaquez !

Right leg forward, right arm stretched out, pretending to hold a sword.

> Ramez !

Find a partner, sit down, pretend to row.

> Nettoyez le bateau !

Pretend to clean the boat with a broom

> Videz le seau !

Pretend to empty a bucket

> Prenez vos boucliers !

Squat down, hold both forearms up to protect the face like a shield

> Trouvez deux (trois, quatre...) Vikings !

Get in groups of three (four, five...)

> Tout le monde à bord !

All sit down in the middle.
Practise these instructions and actions one at a time, build them up gradually using plenty of repetition.
Once the children are familiar with the actions, ask them to run slowly between your commands.

> Courez lentement ! Nettoyez le bateau ! Et courez lentement ! Ramez ! Courez lentement ! Etc.

3. You can use this as a competitive activity in which the last child completing each of the actions is out. Alternatively ask the children to work in groups of four or five to put together a sequence of Viking actions

> Travaillez en groupes de quatre. En groupes, faites une séquence de quatre ou cinq actions.

Allow them time to practise, then ask them to perform

> Maintenant, présentez vos séquences.

4. While each group performs, the other children watch and call out the corresponding commands to go with the actions.

6.3

Education physique

Time guide:	30 minutes + follow-up activities
Content:	Traditional Breton dance
Communication focus:	Language of instructions (dance steps)
Materials needed:	None
Links:	Audio link – instructions for the dance steps, music from www.breizpartitions.fr

Key Stage 2 Framework focus

O 3.4	Use physical response, mime and gesture to convey meaning and show understanding
IU 4.1	Learn about festivals and celebrations in different countries
KAL	Identify specific sounds, phonemes and words
LLS	Use a physical response; play games to help to remember
Languages Ladder	Stage 1 Breakthrough, Grade 2 Listening
Irish Reference	Dance. Strand unit: exploration, creation and performance of dance

Transcription (CD Piste 24)

Aujourd'hui, nous allons apprendre une danse bretonne.
Mettez-vous en cercle, garçon, fille, garçon, fille.
Donnez-vous la main.

Tout le monde fait quatre pas en avant vers le centre du cercle.
Un, deux, trois, quatre.
Tout le monde fait quatre pas en arrière pour retourner aux places d'origine.
Un, deux, trois, quatre.

Les filles, quatre pas en avant vers le centre du cercle.
Les filles, quatre pas en arrière pour retourner aux places d'origine.

Tout le monde fait huit pas.
Un, deux, trois, quatre, cinq, six, sept, huit.

Tout le monde se tourne l'un en face de l'autre.
Tout le monde recule de quatre pas.
Tout le monde avance de quatre pas.

Tout le monde recule de quatre pas.
Tout le monde avance de quatre pas.

Lesson Plan:

1. Start the lesson by explaining that the children are going to learn a Breton dance

> **Aujourd'hui nous allons apprendre une danse bretonne.**

Ask the children to stand in a circle, alternating boy, girl where possible.

> **Mettez-vous en cercle, garçon, fille, garçon, fille.**

Hold hands **Donnez-vous la main.**

2. For the first part of the dance, the whole group moves four steps towards the centre of the circle, then four steps back

> **Tout le monde fait quatre pas en avant vers le centre du cercle. Un, deux, trois, quatre. Tout le monde fait quatre pas en arrière pour retourner aux places d'origine. Un, deux, trois, quatre.**

Next only the girls do the same steps as before

> **Les filles, quatre pas en avant vers le centre du cercle. Les filles, quatre pas en arrière pour retourner aux places d'origine.**

When they return both the girls and the boys take a 90° turn to the right, the couples stand shoulder to shoulder.

3. The second part starts with all the couples moving in the same direction, **la promenade.** Everybody takes eight steps forward, moving around in a circle.

> **Tout le monde fait huit pas.**
> **Un, deux, trois, quatre, cinq, six, sept, huit.**

4. On the last step the couples do a 90° degrees turn, so they end up facing each other.

> **Tout le monde se tourne l'un en face de l'autre.**

Everybody moves four steps back.

> **Tout le monde recule de quatre pas.**

Then four steps towards each other.

> **Tout le monde avance de quatre pas.**

Repeat four steps back,

> **Tout le monde recule de quatre pas.**

then four steps towards each other again.

> **Tout le monde avance de quatre pas.**

On the last steps both partners turn, so they stand shoulder to shoulder again.

Start again with the promenade, all couples moving eight steps forward in a circle etc.
To build in some variations, you can include turning on the spot or a little jump on beat four.

6.4 Education physique

Time guide:	30 minutes
Content:	Games and movement
Communication focus:	Language of instructions and rules
Materials needed:	Ball, marked area
Links:	Audio link – instructions to play the game

Key Stage 2 Framework focus

O 3.3	Perform simple communicative tasks using single words, phrases and short sentences
O 3.4	Listen attentively and understand instructions, everyday classroom language and praise words
KAL	Identify specific sounds, phonemes and words
IU 4.1	Know about some aspects of everyday life and compare them to their own
LLS	Use actions and rhymes and play games to aid memorisation
Languages Ladder	Stage 1 Breakthrough, Grade 2 Listening
Irish Reference	Games. Strand unit: developing ball-handling skills.

Transcription (CD Piste 25)

Aujourd'hui, nous allons jouer un jeu : « Balle au capitaine ».
Nous avons quatre équipes (les rouges, les bleus, les verts et les jaunes)
Chaque équipe a sept joueurs.
Chaque équipe choisit son capitaine.

Deux équipes commencent.
Tous les joueurs sont sur le terrain.
Les deux capitaines sont situés dans leur zone protégée.
Les joueurs passent le ballon.
Chaque équipe doit passer le ballon à son capitaine.

C'est interdit :
les contacts entre les joueurs,
prendre le ballon à quelqu'un,
entrer dans la zone du capitaine,
courir avec le ballon.

Deux points quand le capitaine a reçu le ballon.
Un point pour utiliser le français.

Les phrases pendant le jeu :
Tu as touché...
Tu as pris le ballon.
Tu es dans la zone interdite.
Tu as couru avec le ballon.
Passe-moi le ballon !

Les rouges/verts... ont gagné !

"... à la française" A Cross-curricular Approach to Teaching French at Primary Level © Authentik

Lesson Plan:

1. The game **Balle au capitaine** is similar to benchball and can be played in a hall or outside. It is best to have between 4 and 7 players (plus captain) per team.
Explain to the class that they are going to play a game :

> **Aujourd'hui nous allons jouer un jeu, « Balle au capitaine » .**

Depending on the class size divide the children into teams of 5/6/7 or 8 and give each team a name

> **Nous avons quatre équipes (les rouges, les bleus, les verts et les jaunes). Chaque équipe a sept joueurs.**

Now ask each team to choose a captain **Chaque équipe choisit son capitaine.**

2. Explain the rules of the games using gestures and modelling to support children's comprehension. Two teams start **Deux équipes commencent.** All the players are in the marked out area.

> **Tous les joueurs sont sur le terrain.**

The two captains are in the protected area at both ends.

> **Les deux capitaines sont situés dans leur zone protégée.**

The players pass the ball to each other; the aim is to pass the ball to their captain.

> **Les joueurs passent le ballon. Chaque équipe doit passer le ballon à son capitaine.**

If the players do one of the following moves, the game is interrupted and the opposite team gains possession of the ball. Explain the specific rules to the children by modelling the actions. Not allowed are:

C'est interdit : les contacts entre les joueurs (contact with other players),
prendre le ballon à quelqu'un (snatching the ball from someone),
entrer dans la zone du capitaine (entering the captain's area),
courir avec le ballon (moving while holding the ball).

3. Before you start the game, explain the scoring: two points for the team whose captain catches the ball.

> **Deux points si le capitaine a reçu le ballon.**

1 point every time a player uses a French phrase.

> **Un point pour utiliser le français.**

Write these phrases on the board or a flipchart visible for everybody:

Les phrases pendant le jeu :
Tu as touché…
Tu as pris le ballon.
Tu es dans la zone interdite.
Tu as couru avec le ballon.
Passe-moi le ballon !

4. Start the tournament. Each game should last 5 or ten minutes. The team with most points wins. Announce the winning team.

> **Les rouges/verts… ont gagné !**

7.1

Sciences

Time guide: 30 mins

Content: Group and compare animals, according to what they eat.

Communication focus: Food vocabulary.
Scientific vocabulary for three feeding groups. Carnivore, Herbivore, Omnivore.
Qui mange ....?, Est-ce qu'il mange.....? Qu'est ce que tu aimes manger ?

Materials needed: Food Flashcards. Animal Flashcards, Copymaster 7.1.

Links: Audio link - Pronunciation of food vocabulary

Key Stage 2 Framework focus

O 3.3	Ask and answer questions
L 4.2	Make links between spoken and written words
KAL	Imitate pronunciation of sounds, recognise conventions of politeness
LLS	Play games to remember; use a physical response; practise new language with a friend
Languages Ladder	Stage 1 Breakthrough, Grade 3 Listening and Reading, Grade 2 Speaking, Grade 2 Writing
Irish Reference	Living Things. Strand unit: plant and Animal life. Variety and characteristics of living things.

Transcription (CD Piste 26)

Qu'est ce que tu aimes manger?
Tu es carnivore.
Tu es herbivore.
Qu'est ce qu'il mange? De l'herbe, des feuilles... donc la girafe est herbivore.

Le chien mange des os.
Le mouton mange de l'herbe.
La grenouille mange des insectes.
Le cheval mange des cereales.
Le cochon mange des légumes.
Le tigre mange de la viande.
La girafe mange des plantes.
Le renard mange des petit animaux.
La vache mange de l'herbe.

La vache est herbivore.
Le cochon est omnivore.
Le cheval est herbivore.
Le lion est carnivore.
Le chien est omnivore.
Le chat est carnivore.
Le renard est omnivore.
La girafe est herbivore.
L'oiseau est omnivore.
Je suis
L'ours est omnivore.
Le lapin est herbivore.
La poule est herbivore.
Le tigre est carnivore.
La grenouille est carnivore.

Lesson Plan:

1. Start by asking children what they like to eat. What's their favourite food?

> **Qu'est ce que tu aimes manger ?**

Write the answers on the board.
As you note the answer tell the child

> **Tu es carnivore... ou tu es herbivore.**

See if the children can distinguish what this means.
Decide since we eat both meat and vegetables what are we? Introduce the notion of omnivore.

2. Hold up a picture of a giraffe:

> **Qu'est ce qu'elle mange ?**

> **De l'herbe, des feuilles... donc elle est herbivore.**

and so on with a variety of animals as a whole class activity.

3. Hand out the first copy master, Sciences 7.1
Encourage children to work in pairs or small groups to decide.

> **Qu'est ce qu'ils mangent ?**

The children draw an arrow from one side to the other, remember some animals might eat several of these things.
Next, the children listen to the cassette to hear full sentences being read out, for example:

> **Le chien mange des os.**

Children check their work. Remember different answers are possible.
Now encourage the children to repeat full sentences by asking

> **Qu'est ce que le chien mange ?**   etc

4. Hand out the second page of the copy master Sciences 7.1 Again, ask the children to work in pairs or small groups, next to each animal on the list, they must write either

Carnivore   **Omnivore**   **Herbivore**

Next they listen to the CD Rom to check if their work is correct, and to generate discussion.

5. Finally, and very quickly, flash the animal flashcards and encourage children to call out sentences:

> **Le chien est carnivore.**   etc.

7.2

Sciences

Time guide:	45 mins
Content:	Group and compare living things into sets, according to their similarities and differences. Become familiar with the characteristics of some major groups of living things
Communication focus:	To reinforce animal vocabulary To identify and recognise more scientific vocabulary: *mammifère, reptile* To reinforce question structures: *Qu'est ce que c'est ? Est-ce... ?* To reinforce the structures : *C'est/Ce n'est pas. Il a / Il n'a pas de. Il est/Il n'est pas.*
Materials needed:	Animal Flashcards. Word cards with names of animals, Copy master 7.2.
Links:	Pronunciation of animal vocabulary

Key Stage 2 Framework focus

O 3.3	Ask and answer questions
L 4.2	Make links between spoken and written words
KAL	Recognise question forms and negatives
LLS	Use actions and rhymes and play games to aid memorization; use gestures to show they understand
Languages Ladder	Stage 1 Breakthrough, Grade 2 Listening and Speaking
Irish Reference	Living Things. Strand unit: plant and animal life. Variety and characteristics of living things

Transcription (CD Piste 27)

Qu'est ce que c'est ? C'est un cheval !
la vache, le chien, la souris, le chat, le cochon, le mouton
La famille la plus grande est la famille Mammifère.
Tous les animaux qui font partie de la famille Mammifère ont des caractéristiques en commun.
Ils ont des bébés.
Ils ont des poils.
Ils ont du sang chaud.
Ils produisent du lait pour les petits.

Est-ce un mammifère ?
Le serpent n'est pas un mammifère. Il n'a pas de bébé. Il n'a pas de poil. Il n'a pas de lait. Il a du sang froid.
La famille Reptile.
Ils habitent sur terre et dans l'eau.
Ils pondent des oeufs.
Ils ont du sang froid.

Prenez des feuilles et dessinez un animal

Qui es-tu ? Je suis....

"... à la française"   A Cross-curricular Approach to Teaching French at Primary Level   © Authentik

Lesson Plan:

1. Revisit animals which would be familiar to the children: Using flash-cards ask the children to identify the animal:

Qu'est ce que c'est ?   **C'est un cheval !**

2. Similarly revise the following vocabulary: **la vache, le chien, la souris, le chat, le cochon, le mouton.**

3. Explain that there are animal families. The biggest animal family is the Mammal Family –

La famille la plus grande est la famille Mammifère.
Tous les animaux qui font partie de la famille Mammifère ont des caractéristiques en commun.
Using gesture and mime explain the following characteristics of the Mammal Family

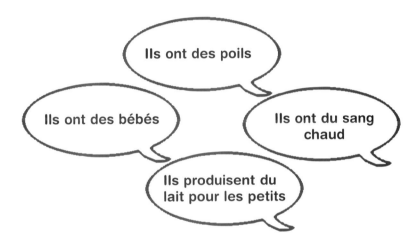

Ils ont des poils

Ils ont des bébés

Ils ont du sang chaud

Ils produisent du lait pour les petits

4. Ask the children if they can think of more mammals. Hold up a flashcard:

Est-ce un mammifère ?

Insert random bird/insect/snake. Explore answers together. Discuss:

Pourquoi le serpent n'est pas un mammifère ?

Il n'a pas de bébé

Il n'a pas de poil

Il a du sang froid

Il n'a pas de lait

5. Introduce the other animal families:

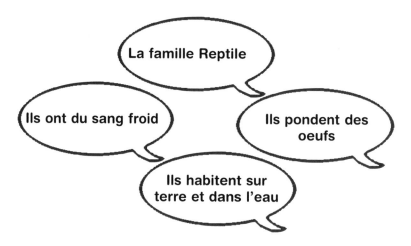

Exemple : **le crocodile**

6. Invite the children to get a piece of loose paper and to draw a picture of an animal, any animal, give them 3 minutes to do this.

Prenez les feuilles et dessinez un animal !

7. Write up three or more headings on the board according to the number of categories you wish to work with:

Mammifère	**Amphibien**	**Insecte**	**Oiseau**	**Reptile**

Invite the children to place their picture under the correct heading.

8. Select four individuals and give them each a category card (from the Copy Master's section at the end of this book), tell them to stand in four different places in the classroom.

Redistribute the children's drawings to the rest of the class (and/or use animal flashcards or the animal sketches at the Copy Master's section of this book.)

Get the children to physically group themselves according to the category they belong to.

Very importantly - before they enter a group they must be asked a question, and then respond before being allowed to enter the group.

Qui es-tu ?   **Je suis...**

Follow-up activities:

You can extend step seven by counting the number in each group. You can do a memory game, children have to close their eyes then list all the creatures that are in one particular group.

Time guide: 30 mins (+30mins follow-on activity)

Content: Investigating and experimenting. The child is enabled to test whether a substance is an acid or an alkali. Red cabbage is an indicator i.e. it is one colour in an acid and it is another in an alkali.

Communication Focus: *Un chou, du jus, de l'eau, un citron, du savon, de la dentifrice. C'est de quelle couleur? Regardez! Ca change de couleur*

Materials needed: See next page, Copy master 7.3.

Links: Audio link

Key Stage 2 Framework focus

O 4.2 **O 3.4**	Listen for specific words and phrases Listen attentively and understand instructions, everyday classroom language and praise words
L 4.2 **L 3.3**	Make links between spoken and written words Write simple familiar words using a model
KAL	Recognise question forms and negatives
LLS	Use gestures to show they understand
Languages Ladder	Stage 1 Breakthrough, Grade 2 Listening and Speaking
Irish Reference	Materials. Strand unit: properties and characteristics of materials

Transcription (CD Piste 28)

Qu'est-ce que c'est ? C'est un chou ! On va couper le chou. On met de l'eau chaude. On attend cinq minutes.
C'est du vinaigre. Est-ce acide ou alcalin ? On va voir ! C'est du bicarbonate du soude. Est-ce acide ou alcalin ? On va voir !
Regardez tout le monde. Le jus est violet. On met du vinaigre.
Mais c'est magique ! Ça change de couleur.
Quelle est la couleur maintenant ? Est-ce acide ou alcalin ?

On met du bicarbonate de soude. Ça change de couleur. Quelle est la couleur maintenant ? Est-ce acide ou alcalin ?
Aidez-moi ! Attention! Doucement !
Dessinez ! Comme c'est joli. Qu'est-ce qui se passe ?
C'est de quelle couleur ? Est-ce acide ou alcalin ?

Materials needed:

Red cabbage, knife, hot water (use a kettle), baking-soda, vinegar, sieve, saucepan, two glass bowls.

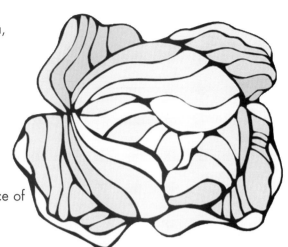

Follow-on activity:

You will need one of the following for each group: large white cloth, droppers, empty yoghurt cartons, orange juice, coca cola, toothpaste, a piece of lemon, soap, newspaper.

Synopsis of experiment

Chop up the red cabbage.

Drop the cabbage into a saucepan of hot water. Leave for a few minutes.

Pour the purple juice through a sieve into the two bowls. Save some cabbage juice for later.

Drip a few drops of vinegar into one bowl.

Sprinkle some bread-soda into the other bowl.

The acid turns the cabbage juice red.

The alkali turns the cabbage juice blue/green.

Background information: Explain to the class that everything is made of chemicals and that chemicals can be sorted into categories. Some are acidic. Some are alkaline and some are neutral. Red cabbage is neutral but it changes colour when it is exposed to an acid or an alkali. It turns red if acid is added and blue or greenish if an alkali is added.

62

Lesson Plan:

1. Hold up the cabbage to the class.

> **Qu'est-ce que c'est ? C'est un chou ! On va couper le chou. On met de l'eau chaude. On attend cinq minutes.**

2. Show the class the bottle of vinegar:

> **C'est du vinaigre. Est-ce acide ou alcalin ? On va voir !**

3. Show the class the tin of baking soda:

> **C'est du bicarbonate du soude.
> Est-ce acide ou alcalin ?
> On va voir !
> Regardez tout le monde.
> Le jus est violet.**

4.

> **On met du vinaigre. Mais c'est magique. Ca change de couleur. Quelle est la couleur maintenant ? Est-ce acide ou alcalin ?**

5.

> **On met du bicarbonate de soude. Ca change de couleur. Quelle est la couleur maintenant ? Est-ce acide ou alcalin ?**

Follow-up activities:

1. Soak the pieces of cloth in the remaining cabbage juice for a few minutes.
Divide the class into groups. Place sheets of newspaper on desks.

2. Enlist some helpers and pour some orange juice/coca cola/squirt of toothpaste/water into separate yoghurt cartons and distribute to each group.
Aidez-moi ! Attention! Doucement !

3. Give each group a purple cloth, a bar of soap and a piece of lemon.
Allow the children to experiment with the different substances and to make patterns of different colours on the cloths using the droppers, the soap and the lemon.
**Dessinez ! Comme c'est joli. Qu'est ce qui se passe ? C'est de quelle couleur ?
Est-ce acide ou alcalin ?**

4. The children should record their results on the grid. Copy master 7.3

7.4

Sciences

Time guide:	30 mins
Content:	To illustrate that magnets produce an invisible force and that some things respond to magnetic force and others do not. To classify objects and formulate hypotheses regarding materials and their magnetic properties
Communication focus:	Vocabulary: everyday objects; Verb: *aimer : Il aime/Il n'aime pas* *Question structure: Est-ce que... C'est / Ce n'est pas*
Materials needed:	You will need the following for each group: a. A bag of objects containing: pencil, rubber, pen, paper-clip, keys, coins, cloth, paper, small plastic ruler, nail, empty tin can, small mirror b. A bar magnet c. Two sheets of paper, different colours, labelled "Magnétique" and "Non-Magnétique"
Links:	Audio link

Key Stage 2 Framework focus

O 4.2 **O 3.4**	Listen for specific words and phrases Use physical response, mime and gesture to convey meaning and show understanding
L 4.4	Write simple words and phrases using a model and some words from memory
KAL	Reinforce and extend recognition of word classes and understand their function
LLS	Use mental associations to help remember words
Languages Ladder	Stage 1 Breakthrough, Grade 2 Listening and Speaking
Irish Reference	Energy and Forces. Strand unit: magnetism.

Transcription (CD Piste 29)

Qu'est-ce que j'ai dans mon sac ? J'ai un crayon. J'ai un stylo. J'ai une gomme, une règle, du papier, un trombone, des clés, une pièce, un chiffon, un clou, une boîte, un miroir. Montrez-moi un clou ! Montrez-moi une gomme ! Montrez-moi une boîte ! un aimant, aimer, il/elle aime il/elle n'aime pas Quels objets vont aimer l'aimant ? La boîte aime l'aimant. Le miroir n'aime pas l'aimant. Magnétique, Non-Magnétique.

Regardez ! C'est magnétique. Ce n'est pas magnétique. Quels objets aiment l'aimant ? Est-ce que le trombone est magnétique ? Oui, c'est magnétique. Est-ce que le chiffon est magnétique ? Non, ce n'est pas magnétique. Combien d'objets magnétiques y a-t-il ? Combien d'objets non-magnétiques y a-t-il ? Est-ce que les objets en métal sont tous magnétiques ? Est-ce que les objets en plastique sont tous magnétiques ? Est-ce que les objets en bois sont tous magnétiques ?

"... à la française"   A Cross-curricular Approach to Teaching French at Primary Level   © Authentik

Lesson Plan:

1. Invite the children to guess what is in your bag.

> Qu'est-ce que j'ai dans mon sac ?

Reveal the contents one by one.

> J'ai un crayon. J'ai un stylo. J'ai une gomme, une règle, du papier, un trombone, des clés, une pièce, un chiffon, un clou, une boîte, un miroir.

2. Divide the class into groups of four. Pass out a bag of materials to each group. To ensure comprehension of the new vocabulary ask the children to show you an object.

> Montrez-moi un clou! Montrez-moi une gomme ! Montrez-moi une boîte !

3. Introduce the magnet. Draw children's attention to the French word: un aimant and the link with the word aimer

Draw a big love-heart on one side of the board and write the word il/elle aime underneath.

On the other side draw a big love-heart with a cross through it and write il/elle n'aime pas underneath.

4. As a class, ask learners to predict which objects will be attracted to the magnet.

> Quels objets vont aimer l'aimant ?

Record the children's predictions on the board.

> La boîte aime l'aimant. Le miroir n'aime pas l'aimant.

5. Introduce the terms **Magnétique** and **Non-Magnétique**. Give each group a magnet and two sheets of coloured paper marked **Magnétique** and **Non-Magnétique**.
6. Each group experiments with the objects in the bag to determine if they are magnetic or not. As each item is tested, learners sort the objects into two groups by placing them on the appropriate sheet.

> Regardez ! C'est magnétique. Ce n'est pas magnétique.

7. After the groups have completed the activity, bring the class together for discussion:

> Quels objets aiment l'aimant ?

> Est-ce que le trombone est magnétique? Oui, c'est magnétique.

> Est-ce que le chiffon est magnétique? Non, ce n'est pas magnétique.

> Combien d'objets magnétiques y a-t-il ?

> Combien d'objets non-magnétiques y a-t-il ?

> Est-ce que les objets en métale sont tous magnétiques ?

> Est-ce que les objets en plastique sont tous magnétiques ?

> Est-ce que les objets en bois sont tous magnétiques ?

8. Invite children to fill out the grid. Copy master 7.4

Copy Masters

26	**18**	**16**
10	**20**	
		14

sept	**vingt-six**	**onze**
4 + 6 + 16	5 + 6	22 + 9
trente-et-un	**dix**	**dix-sept**
5 + 6 - 1	8 + 9	14 + 8
vingt-deux	**trente**	**vingt-quatre**
22 + 8	9 + 8 + 7	34 + 8
quarante-deux	**soixante**	**cinquante**
30 + 20 + 10	24 + 26	60 - 53

Place les cases sur le quadrillage. Colorie les cases.

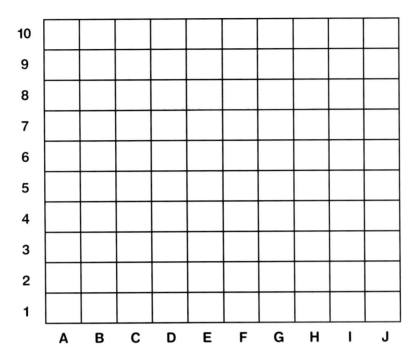

Travaille avec un partenaire.

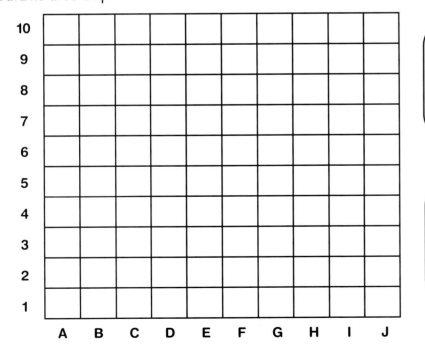

A

C7, E7, C2, E2, D5, C6,
C3, C4, E4, E6, D4, E3

B

E8, D6, B8, B4, E6, C8, B6,
B7, C4, D8, E4, E5, D4, B5

Trouve les paires.

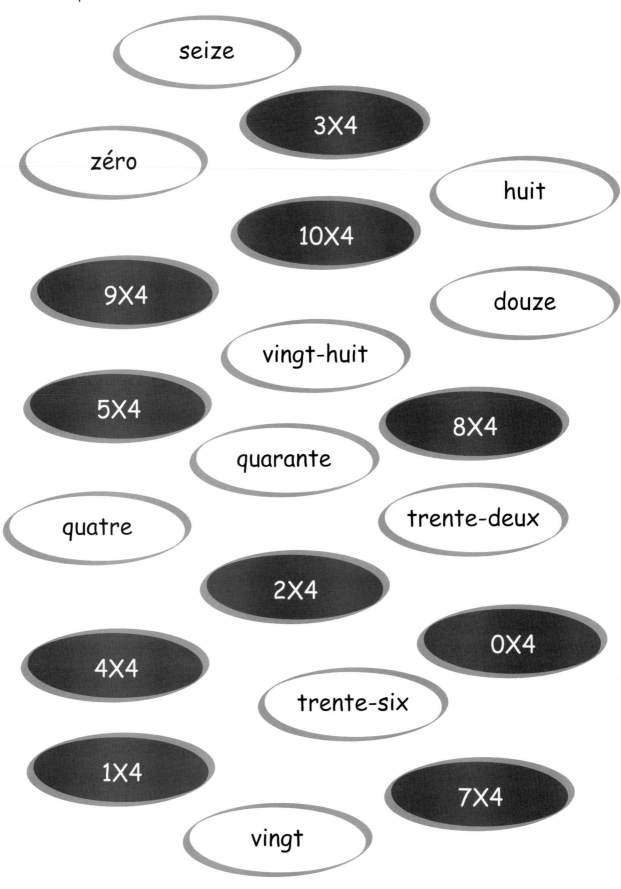

seize

3X4

zéro

huit

10X4

9X4

douze

vingt-huit

5X4

8X4

quarante

quatre

trente-deux

2X4

0X4

4X4

trente-six

1X4

7X4

vingt

C'est quel nombre ?

1. Je pense à un nombre..........

On peut le diviser par sept.
On peut le diviser par cinq.
Il y a deux chiffres.
Le deuxième chiffre est 0.

C'est quel nombre ?

2. Je pense à un nombre..........

On peut le diviser par neuf.
On peut le diviser par cinq.
Il y a trois chiffres.
Le premier chiffre est 1.
Le troisième chiffre est 0.

C'est quel nombre ?

3. Je pense à un nombre..........

On peut le diviser par _____.
On peut le diviser par _____.
Il y a _____ chiffres.
Le _____ chiffre est _____.

C'est quel nombre ?

4. Je pense à un nombre..........

C'est un nombre premier.
Si on multiplie le nombre par cinq et par trois, ça fait un nombre entre 250 et 260.
Si on divise ce nombre par 10, ça fait un nombre entre 25.4 et 25.6.

C'est quel nombre ?

La monnaie

Pour payer exactement ces sommes, avec le moins de pièces et de billets possibles, que doit-on donner?

Exemple: 45,20 € - 2 billets de 20 €, 1 billet de 5 €, 1 pièce de 20 c.

17,60 €

_____

_____

_____

_____

65,15 €

_____

_____

_____

_____

29,99 €

_____

_____

_____

91,73 €

_____

_____

_____

Bienvenue à Disneyland Paris !
Une famille, deux adultes et trois enfants, visite Disneyland Paris.
Ils veulent rester un jour et ils veulent visiter un parc.
Ça fait combien d'euros ?

La France en Europe

Fais le quiz des pays européens.

1. Quel pays est situé entre l'Allemagne et l'Italie ?

l'Autriche ❑
le Portugal ❑
le Danemark ❑
l'Espagne ❑

2. Quel pays est situé au sud du Danemark ?

la France ❑
la Suède ❑
l'Allemagne ❑
le Royaume-Uni ❑

3. Quel pays est situé au nord-est de la France ?

la Belgique ❑
l'Italie ❑
la Grèce ❑
l'Espagne ❑

4. Les deux pays qui ne touchent pas la France sont…

la Suisse et l'Espagne ❑
l'Irlande et l'Autriche ❑
la Belgique et l'Italie ❑

5. Quel est le pays le plus grand ?

l'Autriche ❑
la Grèce ❑
le Danemark ❑
la France ❑

6. Quel est le pays le plus petit ?

la Belgique ❑
la Suisse ❑
l'Irlande ❑
le Luxembourg ❑

7. Quel pays a plus d'habitants que la France ? _____

8. Les capitales de ces pays sont……

la France _____
la Belgique _____
l'Espagne _____

La France en Europe

Danemark
5,4 millions d'habitants

Royaume-Uni
59,9 millions d'habitants

Irlande
4,2 millions d'habitants

Belgique
10,5 millions d'habitants

Allemagne
82,5 millions d'habitants

Luxembourg
0,4 millions d'habitants

France
64 millions d'habitants

Autriche
8,1 millions d'habitants

Suisse
7,5 millions d'habitants

Portugal
10,6 millions d'habitants

Espagne
44,7 millions d'habitants

Italie
58,7 millions d'habitants

Grèce
10,6 millions d'habitants

Les monuments de Paris

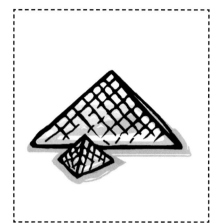

C'est une église.	C'est un musée.	La construction a duré de 1163 à 1345.
C'est une tour.	La hauteur est de 324 mètres.	Il a été construit en 1594.
La construction a duré de 1887 à 1889.	Il y a plus de 6 millions de visiteurs par an.	Il y a plus de 8 millions de visiteurs par an.
Elle a été construite par Gustave Eiffel.	Ici on peut voir La Joconde de Léonard de Vinci.	Il y a plus de 12 millions de visiteurs par an.
La hauteur est de 69 mètres.	La tour a été construite avec 18 038 pièces métalliques.	« J'aime l'art. »
« Je suis sportif ! Je prends l'escalier ! »	« J'aime l'histoire. »	La pyramide à l'entrée fait 21 mètres de haut.

Paris et La Réunion – Saisons et climat

Compare les diagrammes et remplis les blancs:

La température est plus élevée à Paris au mois de ……….. et ………… et ……………

La température est plus élevée à La Réunion au mois de ……….. et ………… et ……

La température la plus élevée à Paris est ……………….degrés.

La température la plus élevée à La Réunion est ……………….degrés.

Au mois de janvier, il y a ………………….mm de pluie à Paris, mais il y a
………………………….mm de pluie à La Réunion.

Pourquoi, c'est different ?

A La Réunion il y a un climat …………………………

Paris est dans l'hémisphère ……………….., La Réunion est dans l'hémisphère
…………………………………

Nord	Sud	juin	52	août
tropical	janvier	25	février	
32	140	juillet	mars	

printemps	été	automne	hiver

janvier	février	mars	avril

mai	juin	juillet	août

septembre	octobre	novembre	décembre

3.1

Les instruments de l'orchestre

Quels instruments sont dans le groupe ....
(Choisis la même couleur pour chaque groupe et ses instruments)

des percussions

des cuivres

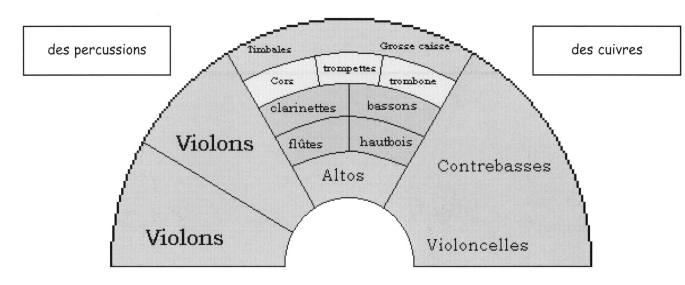

des cordes

des bois

Mes instruments préférés

J'adore le son <u>du/de la/des</u> ....

J'aime aussi le son <u>du/de la/des</u> ....

Je déteste le son <u>du/de la/des</u> ....

Je voudrais jouer ....

Je joue déjà ....

du violon	de la contrebasse	des timbales
du violoncelle	de la flûte	des cymbales
du cor	de la clarinette	
du basson	de la trompette	
du trombone	de la grosse caisse	
du hautbois		

Les instruments de l'orchestre

Les cordes

le violon

le violoncelle

la contrebasse

Les bois

la flûte

le hautbois

la clarinette

le basson

Les cuivres

le cor

la trompette

le trombone

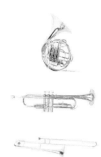

Les percussions

la grosse caisse

les timbales

les cymbales

<u>Travaillez en groupe de quatre.</u>

Utilisez les phrases et les actions pour créer le son.

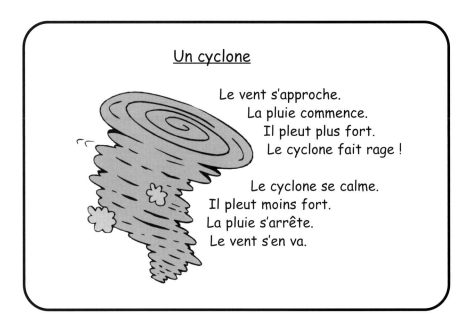

Un cyclone

Le vent s'approche.
La pluie commence.
Il pleut plus fort.
Le cyclone fait rage !

Le cyclone se calme.
Il pleut moins fort.
La pluie s'arrête.
Le vent s'en va.

<u>Un bâton de pluie</u>

Attention ! Seulement sous surveillance

Matériel: un rouleau en carton
des graines
du carton et du papier
du scotch
un marteau et des clous

1. Prends le rouleau de carton. Prends le marteau. Plante les clous dans le rouleau.

2. Bouche un côté du rouleau avec un morceau de carton en forme de rond (au diamètre du rouleau).

3. Mets des graines dans le rouleau. Bouche l'autre côté du rouleau avec un deuxième morceau de carton en forme de rond.

4. Décore le bâton de pluie.

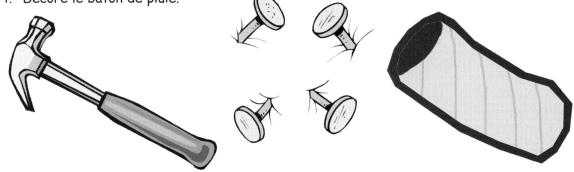

A la manière d'Henri Matisse

Découpe des formes droites et des formes arrondies.

Prends la colle. Colle les formes sur le papier.

Prends les ciseaux.

Prends le papier et la boîte de peintures.

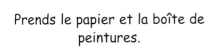

Et voilà, c'est fini !

Colorie le papier.

Avec toutes les formes, fais ta composition.

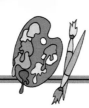

Concours : Faites un pont !

Aujourd'hui vous allez faire un projet. Vous allez faire la maquette d'un pont.

Voici les instructions.

Faites un pont en groupes de quatre

Vous avez 4 feuilles de papier, 4 feuilles de carton, 15 pailles, des ciseaux, du scotch

Vous allez utiliser quels matériels ? Discutez et choisissez !

Décidez : le pont est en bois, en fer ou en pierre ? Le pont est pour les véhicules ou pour les piétons ?

Maintenant, faites la maquette !

Attention ! Quand vous avez fini, vérifiez la stabilité de votre pont. Placez une balle de tennis sur le pont – le pont est cassé, oui ou non ?

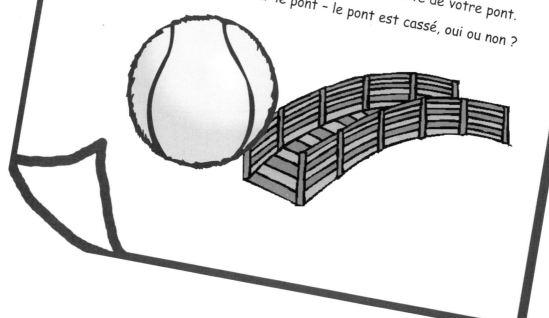

Au marché des Vikings

J'ai donné...		J'ai reçu...
	un vase	
	une broche	
	une épée	
	une cuillère	
	un bateau	
	un collier	
	un verre	
	un peigne	
	des chaussures	

Au marché des Vikings j'ai donné...

_____

_____

_____

Au marché des Vikings j'ai reçu

_____

_____

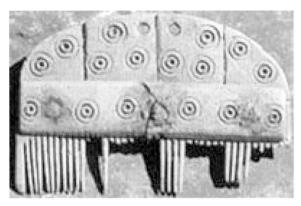

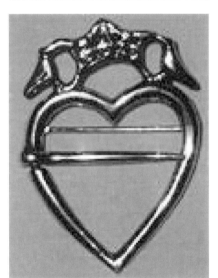

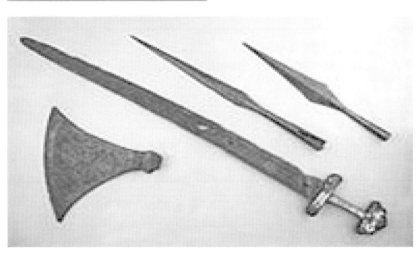

Les enfants du 19ème siècle

Qu'est-ce qu'il pense ? Ecris des phrases.

Je suis fatigué !	Où est maman ?
Je suis triste !	J'ai soif !
J'ai chaud !	J'habite dans une grande maison avec douze chambres.
J'ai beaucoup de jouets.	J'ai peur !
J'ai faim !	Le travail est dangereux.
Je mange beaucoup de bonbons.	Je veux jouer avec mes amis !

Les enfants du 19ème siècle

<u>Trouve les paires qui rimest.</u>

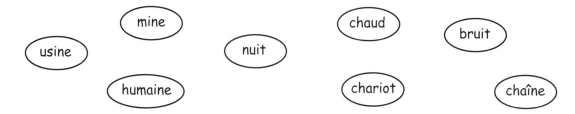

mine

chaud

bruit

usine

nuit

humaine

chariot

chaîne

<u>Lis le poème et remplis les blancs.</u>

Un poème

Tourne, machine, tourne
jour et nuit.
Tourne, machine, ...
trop trop de ....!

Pousse, garçon, ...
ton chariot.
Pousse dans la mine
dangereuse; il fait ....!

Rêve, enfant, rêve,
enfant en chaînes.
..................., enfant, rêve,
d'une vie plus ....!

humaine	tourne	chaud
pousse	rêve	bruit

Les animaux et la nourriture

Qu'est ce qu'ils mangent ?

le chien

le mouton

la grenouille

le cheval

le cochon

le tigre

la girafe

le renard

la vache

des plantes

de l'herbe

de la viande

des os

des céréales

des insectes

des légumes

des fruits

des petits animaux

		Carnivore	Omnivore	Herbivore
la vache				
le cochon				
le cheval				
le lion				
le chien				
le chat				
le renard				
la girafe				
l'oiseau				
toi !				
l'ours				
le lapin				
la poule				
le tigre				
la grenouille				

 Le mouton

 Le cochon

 Le chat

 Le tigre

 L'ours

 La girafe

 La grenouille

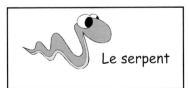 Le serpent

 L'arraignée

 La vache

 La poule

 Le chien

 Le lion

 Le singe

 L'éléphant

La baleine

 Le crocodile

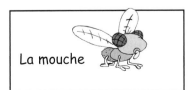 La mouche

Mammifère

Amphibien

Reptile

Insecte

Oiseau

Objet	Couleur	Acide	Alcalin	Neutre

	Magnétique	Non-magnétique